The Military History
of the Bicycle

To my granddaughters Harriett and Olivia,
with whom I've enjoyed many bicycle rides.

The Military History of the Bicycle

The Forgotten War Machine

John Norris

Pen & Sword
MILITARY

First published in Great Britain in by
Pen & Sword Military
An imprint of
Pen & Sword Books Ltd
Yorkshire – Philadelphia

Copyright © John Norris 2021

ISBN 978 1 52676 351 8

The right of John Norris to be identified as Author of this work has been
asserted by him in accordance with the Copyright, Designs and Patents
Act 1988.

Printed and bound in the UK by CPI Group (UK) Ltd,
Croydon, CR0 4YY.

Pen & Sword Books Limited incorporates the imprints of Atlas,
Archaeology, Aviation, Discovery, Family History, Fiction, History,
Maritime, Military, Military Classics, Politics, Select, Transport, True
Crime, Air World, Frontline Publishing, Leo Cooper, Remember When,
Seaforth Publishing, The Praetorian Press, Wharncliffe Local History,
Wharncliffe Transport, Wharncliffe True Crime and White Owl.

For a complete list of Pen & Sword titles please contact

PEN & SWORD BOOKS LIMITED
47 Church Street, Barnsley, South Yorkshire, S70 2AS, England
E-mail: enquiries@pen-and-sword.co.uk
Website: www.pen-and-sword.co.uk

Or
PEN AND SWORD BOOKS
1950 Lawrence Rd, Havertown, PA 19083, USA
E-mail: Uspen-and-sword@casematepublishers.com
Website: www.penandswordbooks.com

The more I see of war, the more I realise how it all depends upon administration and transportation

Field Marshal Lord Wavell

Contents

Acknowledgements		ix
Introduction		xi
Chapter 1	The Idea Takes Shape	1
Chapter 2	Armies find their Wheels 1888–1914	10
Chapter 3	Tyre Treads 1914–18	25
Chapter 4	Wheels and Wings	43
Chapter 5	The Great War Continues	57
Chapter 6	Other Services Needed Bicycles	71
Chapter 7	Evacuation of the Wounded	76
Chapter 8	America Fights and the End of the War	84
Chapter 9	The Wheels Turn Again 1930–45	86
Chapter 10	Wheels Turn West: Blitzkrieg 1940	103
Chapter 11	Hitler's Allies	116
Chapter 12	Britain Stands Alone	118
Chapter 13	The Wheels Move East: Other Theatres of War	138
Chapter 14	Second Front: The Allies Return to Europe	144
Chapter 15	The Battle for Berlin	162
Chapter 16	Wheels in the Cold War	167
Chapter 17	A Modern Trend	174
References and Bibliography		179
Index		181

Acknowledgements

I would like to express my sincere gratitude to the many people who have assisted me in compiling this work, by supplying images, answering my questions and various emails and giving so freely of their time. Firstly, to my very good friend Chris Lay, thank you for supplying images of the cap badges for the Army Cyclist Corps. Thanks also Andrew Watson and Charles Skinner for answering so many questions. I am grateful to the National Cycle Collection in Wales where the staff answered my emails and identified a most unusual object. To the many and various owners of bicycles I spotted at military shows, thank you for allowing me to photograph your machines. And to all the re-enactors and owners of vintage bicycles who gave their time so freely to arrange photographs, I extend my sincere gratitude.

Introduction

Despite the adage that an army marches on its stomach, the simple fact is that it marches on its feet. Over the centuries it has been proved that whoever moves their troops fastest gains the edge over his opponent. Unfortunately, moving fast does have the effect of tiring the troops on the march, but by being in place first allows some time to recover and, more importantly, the opportunity to deploy one's troops in good order. Speed is of the essence in war, but to move fast, and over a long distance, an army must have strength and stamina to keep going. Throughout history, armies across the world used many modes of transport during their campaigns, from camels to horse-drawn wagons, until arriving at the point of motorised transportation. Towards the end of the nineteenth century another mode of transportation was added to that list in the shape of the bicycle. Requiring neither fuel or fodder, and capable of remaining operational with only basic maintenance, it was to show itself to be more economical than any other method of transportation and come to prove its worth many times over.

Armies have completed feats of incredible endurance by marching great distances to engage in battle. During the campaigns of the Napoleonic Wars all armies marched everywhere, from Spain to Russia and Italy to Sweden. One of the greatest feats of endurance of any military campaign, either before or since, began on 24 June 1812, when Napoleon Bonaparte, leading an army of over 600,000 men and 200,000 horses, invaded Russia in the most ambitious campaign of his military career. Over the coming weeks his army advanced further, the Russian army avoided battle, and any engagement was far from being conclusive. As the Russians retreated, they destroyed everything that could be useful to the French, including all food stocks and fodder for the horses.

On 14 September Napoleon entered the city of Moscow, having marched his army more than 500 miles. The victory was to be short-lived, because fire broke out and the city was destroyed, forcing the French, with little in the way of supplies, to leave in mid-October. By now winter had set in and the remains of his army struggled to retreat in harsh conditions. The last of the troops made their way back in early 1813. Napoleon had marched his army over 1,000 miles on a campaign which lost him more than 500,000 troops and was, in the end, all for nothing.

In 1908, 104 years after the Moscow debacle, the British army announced the formation of a new mobile force made up of cyclist troops formed into battalions. The unit comprised several thousand infantrymen riding bicycles, each of which could cover up to fifty miles a day, carrying the burden of his equipment on the same machine. The creation of this new force arose from successful field trials over twenty years earlier which proved the bicycle had a useful military application. The infantry now had a new and independent mode of transportation, but the force was not to remain alone for long because several European armies were creating similar bicycle forces, including France and Belgium.

The idea was picked up further afield. The Japanese and Russian armies investigated the potential of the bicycle, and in America soldiers engaged in a marathon military exercise to demonstrate the usefulness of the machine by riding bicycles to travel almost 2,000 miles in forty days, an average of 50 miles a day.

The first practical bicycle was developed in the early nineteenth century and it was not long before its value to the military was recognised. In fact, within only a very short time bicycles were in limited service with several armies, being viewed as cheap, effective means of transportation for the infantry. During the Franco-Prussian War of 1870–71 French army messengers rode machines known as 'velocipedes' to carry orders between units. However, it was not until the Second Boer War of 1899–1902, that the British army and the Boers proved how useful bicycles could be in war, with both sides using them as transportation and as means to transport supplies and equipment. By the end of the twentieth century, the bicycle would be used in warfare on six continents.

Like other innovations, once the influential armies of the world, such as the British, French and Prussian, led the way in the use of bicycles, other armies were quick to follow. Using bicycles, soldiers could cover many miles without becoming overtired and transport surprisingly heavy loads to keep them operational in the field. The bicycle was something even the smaller armies could afford, and countries such as Spain, Portugal and Belgium saw the benefits of using bicycles to move troops. As the years passed so the importance of the bicycle continued to increase so that by the outbreak of the First World War in 1914, several European armies had cyclist units and the British army had formed whole battalions in the Cyclist Corps.

When the war ended in 1918, sales of bicycles to the military continued. One such country to continue this trend was Japan. When Japan attacked China in 1937, Japanese troops used perhaps as many as 50,000 bicycles during the invasion. Four years later each infantry division of the Japanese army was issued with 6,000 bicycles as the country made final preparations for war in 1941.

The role of the bicycle during the Second World War was still very strong and in 1939 several European armies were equipped with the machines. Even as late as 1944, some of the most dramatic photographic images are those showing British and Canadian troops wading ashore on Sword and Juno beaches in Normandy on D-Day carrying bicycles. When Britain created the Home Guard, renamed from the Local Defence Volunteers raised in 1940, the men serving in these units often used privately-owned bicycles for mobility and to extend the range of their patrols.

It was not just the military which used bicycles. Female civilian organizations such as the Women's Institute, the Women's Voluntary Service and the Women's Land Army also used them to go about their duties. Police officers used them to patrol as 'Bobby on the beat' and Air Raid Precaution Wardens and Civil Defence volunteers rode bicycles to either warn of an air raid or give the all clear.

The German army was making extensive use of bicycles even before hostilities broke out in 1939. One pre-war movement to use bicycles as transport was the paramilitary organization known as the *Reichsarbeitsdienst* or RAD (Reich Labour Corps), which had been raised during the rearmament period and employed on public works projects building bridges and roads.

By the end of the Second World War, which had ushered in the use of jet aircraft, long-range ballistic rockets and the atomic bomb, the humble bicycle was still proving itself useful. During the many post-war conflicts, regular and irregular troops found bicycles most useful machines. For example, in the Vietnam War of the 1960s and 1970s, brigades of Viet Cong troops of the North Vietnamese army used tens of thousands of bicycles to transport food, ammunition and supplies through the jungle to reach the fighting troops. Indeed, it has been opined that without this line of logistical support the Viet Cong could not have maintained their operations against the American and South Vietnamese army. Despite its humble appearance the bicycle has proved itself many times to be an essential piece of military equipment.

Hundreds of bicycle units have been formed in the armies of many countries, so many in fact that it is not possible to mention each one in turn within the space of this work. Not all companies lasted and not all designs they produced proved to be useful to the military. Therefore only those companies which worked closely with their national army and those designs which proved successful or adaptable to be of use in war are included here. Likewise, the growing trend to develop electrically-powered bicycles is not covered and the main theme will adhere to the telling of the history of pedal bicycles in military service.

In conclusion, to assess the contribution made by cyclist units, one only needs to look among the graves in the British Commonwealth War Grave Commission cemeteries from the First World War to see the headstones of the men who served with units such as the British Army Cyclist Corps, or the names on the memorials to those with no-known-grave such as Tyne Cot in Belgium. Cyclist units are also included on Divisional memorials, such as that to the British army's 14th Light Division at Hill 60 near Zillebeke, and that to the cyclists of the Belgian army near Haelen.

Chapter 1

The Idea Takes Shape

Like many great inventions which have changed the world, the bicycle underwent many stages of development before it evolved to reach its modern form. The first serious attempt to produce a bicycle appeared in 1816 when the German inventor Baron Karl von Drais revealed a wooden frame mounted on two wheels fixed in line one behind the other. Sometimes known as the 'Draisienne' after its inventor, the rider sat astride, positioned on a seat and holding a handle to steady himself, the device was propelled by the rider using his feet in a running action while remaining seated. This method of propulsion led to it also being known as the *Laufmaschine* (running machine).

Over the next fifty years further designs were developed, but it was not until the early 1860s that a series of improvements would finally set things in the right direction which would lead towards the development of a serviceable machine. The first of these came about when two French craftsmen, Pierre Lallement and Pierre Michaux refined the concept of the bicycle with the introduction of a mechanical crank, whereby the rider could use the power of his legs to propel pedals fitted to the front wheel which kept the machine in motion. Further refinements and inventions soon followed with individual engineers tackling problems which improved on the overall working of the bicycle. One of the most important of these was undoubtedly the idea to remove the pedal crank from the front wheel and place the pedals directly under the centreline of the rider's seat. This allowed the method of propulsion to be transferred to the rear wheel by means of a chain.

By the mid-nineteenth century the wooden frames of the early designs were being replaced by constructions using tubular steel which were more durable and stronger. From the engineers' and mechanics' point of view, these metal frames were better for the application of inventions. At around this time, the term bicycle was being used in the French popular press. The expression caught on and was soon widely used in overseas newspapers from where the word entered everyday speech.

One of the earliest trials to produce the rear wheel method of pedalling had been conducted by Thomas McCall in 1869. His idea showed how the concept freed the front wheel of any attachments which would impede steering and improve the ability to change direction while still pedalling to keep moving. The rider could now continue to pedal, and with better control of the bicycle, direction could be changed quickly and through a tighter turning radius. By 1888 the chain-drive method which connected the frame-mounted pedal cranks to the rear wheel had been universally adopted. A French designer, Eugène Meyer, made improvements to the wheels by developing wire spokes which lightened the wheels with little or no compromise to either rigidity or strength. Proper handlebars, which formed a 'T-shaped' juncture over the front wheel, gave the rider an improved method of steering and better control.

Further innovations followed, such as the introduction in 1888 of the pneumatic tyre, which had an inflated rubber inner tube to provide a cushioning effect on uneven road surfaces. Developed by Scots-born John Boyd Dunlop, a veterinarian surgeon by training but with an interest in inventing, the new tyre complemented the spoked wheel and would also be adopted by the nascent motor car industry. Gearing mechanisms and braking systems were introduced to enable the bicycle to both go faster and slow down. Entrepreneurs, such as Englishman Rowley Turner, saw business opportunities and established the first factories to meet the demand for the new form of transportation.

In 1868, Turner was working for the Coventry Sewing Machine Company as a sales representative when he acquired a bicycle produced in France by Pierre Michaux, a blacksmith turned bicycle manufacturer. Together with his uncle Josiah Turner, and a business partner, James Starley, Turner established a bicycle factory in Coventry to meet the growing demand for this innovative mode of transport. More factories manufacturing bicycles followed, such as the Nottingham-based Raleigh Bicycle Company, established in 1888. In France, the company of Peugeot was established in 1882 to manufacture bicycles, which during the First World War would diversify and, in addition to producing 62,000 bicycles annually, also produced 9,000 motor vehicles, 1,000 motorcycles, aircraft engines and ammunition for the French army. In 1862 Adam Opel established his factory in Russelsheim in Germany producing sewing machines. In 1886, the company joined the growing number of bicycle manufacturers by diversifying into their production and then branching into the production of motorcars. By the 1920s, Opel would become the single largest manufacturer of bicycles in the world, but collectively Britain's factories produced the most of any country at the turn of the nineteenth century.

The British company of Birmingham Small Arms, BSA, had been founded in 1861 with the aim of manufacturing weapons for military and civilian markets, but by 1869 it had diversified to produce bicycles. Within ten years the company was receiving orders to produce ever more machines to keep up with demand. At first, these designs were built under licence, such as the 'Otto Dicycle'. However, by 1881 BSA was producing bicycles of its own design. Despite the popularity and very good sales, it was to be a short-lived interest in bicycles for BSA. In 1887 the company halted bicycle manufacture and concentrated instead on its primary role of manufacturing armaments.

BSA did not entirely give up its business interests in manufacturing bicycles however. From around 1894 the company was producing components for other companies manufacturing bicycles, and between 1901 and 1911 BSA returned to bicycle manufacturing to supply machines to the British army for the battalions of the newly raised Cyclist Corps. During the First World War, BSA supplied both motorcycles and bicycles to the army and police forces across Britain, as well as producing rifles and machine guns. In 1915, for the Middle East campaign, conducted across Egypt and the regions then known as Salonika and Mesopotamia (modern-day Greece and Iraq), the British army was supplied with nearly 1,500 bicycles by BSA. To meet the growing demand for bicycles, not only by the British army but other armies as well, BSA took on an additional 10,000 staff, of which fifteen per cent were women. After the Partition of Ireland in 1922, BSA would continue to produce and supply bicycles for the newly formed Army of the Irish Republic. During the Second World War, the company supplied around half of all the machines used by the British army.

By the closing years of the nineteenth century, the modern bicycle had arrived and, apart from some variations such as size of wheels or shape of frame, most designs had taken on a form which was universally recognised. As well as the horse or horse-drawn wagon, the ordinary person, provided they could afford a machine, now had the means to move independently and cover greater distances than on foot. It was just a question of time before the value the bicycle offered was realised and it joined the horse and the railway as a means of transport for the military. This recognition came before the turn of the century with several armies conducting exercises with troops using bicycles to prove the potential of the machines in war.

As the twentieth century progressed, the popularity of the bicycle continued to grow, largely because of the means it provided for the ordinary person to move independently. This popularity led to the foundation of more companies to produce ever more machines. For example, the Coventry-based company of Rudge was founded in 1894 and the Stratford-upon-Avon-based company of Pashley, in Warwickshire, was founded in 1926. Bicycle manufacturing companies were also springing up in America and across Europe. In France by 1892 there were an estimated 10,000 people riding machines manufactured by the company of Michelin alone. Other French bicycle manufacturers, such as Peugeot, and Renault, could report similar enthusiasm for their machines.

The popularity of the bicycle was reflected in the hundreds of civilian cycling clubs springing up in Britain, France and America with thousands of members, as people saw the benefits the machines provided for them to better enjoy their leisure time and also for sporting contests. Manufacturers arranged exhibitions where their designs and developments could be showcased. In several countries, specialist venues known as National Cycle Shows were held which companies from around the world could attend. At first in their hundreds, the number of exhibitors increased to thousands as they displayed a range of conventional designs from the standard two-wheeled machines through to tandems which could be ridden by two people. Even the tricycle, despite its old-fashioned appearance, would prove to have an application in the military during the wars which lay ahead. A range of publications sprang up, such as the British magazine *Cycling Weekly*, first published in 1891 for cycling enthusiasts. These passed on news, reviews and details of organised events and shows, such as the National Cycle Shows and competitive races for speed and endurance.

The exhibitions attracted some strange suggestions. For example, at one Royal Military Tournament in London a specialist bicycle design was exhibited at a stand sponsored by Messrs Wyckoff, Seamans & Bendick, proprietors of the Remington Standard Typewriter. It was a standard bicycle to the handlebars of which was attached a typewriter. The combination was seriously proposed for use by war correspondents, providing both a means of transportation and a typewriter for journalists to compose their dispatches. It attracted mixed interest. Several noted dignitaries saw the machine, including the Duke of Cambridge and the Princess of Wales, to whom a member of staff demonstrated how it might work.

At Crystal Palace quadricycles were exhibited with machine guns mounted on the handlebars. Unsound as these may have seemed, they would inspire other designers to conceive more practical machines. As the historian Colin Kirsch mentions in his *Bad Teeth no Bar*: 'There were no motorized vehicles yet, and cycles had developed into a practical form.' However, that situation was not destined to last for much longer.

In 1879 the German engineer Karl Benz, with a long-time interest in bicycles and already an established business in repairing them, was granted a patent for his internal combustion engine which used petroleum spirit distilled from crude oil as fuel. Several years later Benz was granted a patent for his invention of a motorised vehicle known as the 'Benz patent Motorwagen' which used one of his engines mounted on a tricycle frame fitted with metal-rimmed metal-spoked wheels to support the tyres from the hub, similar in design to the wheels used on bicycles. In that same year, 1885, Benz was joined by fellow German engineer Gottlieb Daimler, who had separately developed his own design for an engine which also used petroleum spirit as a fuel. These early internal combustion engines promised automotive power on a scale never before imagined, and one of the first customers to purchase a machine of Benz's design was Émile Roger, a French bicycle manufacturer based in Paris.

The first models of these vehicles were relatively low powered, around 3.5 hp, but they grabbed the attention of other engineers leading to further developments. In 1899, using a de Dion Bouton four-wheeled vehicle, looking not unlike a quadricycle, German-born engineer and associate of Gottlieb Daimler, Frederick Richard Simms, demonstrated his idea to give mobility to the first belt-fed machine guns by mounting one forward of the steering handle bars. He called the design the 'Motor Scout' and hoped to interest the British army.

By now resident in Britain, he followed up his idea three years later with the 'War Car', a motorised vehicle mounting machine guns and protected by armoured plate. There were other similar vehicles being proposed at the time, including those designed by Dvinitsky and Lutski in Russia, and those of American inventor Edward Joel Pennington. Ideas for such machines would be developed to eventually become motorbikes and cars, and ultimately armoured vehicles. This left the bicycle untouched and able to continue down its own path.

Horses had for centuries provided the means of large-scale movement for armies, not only to transport troops, but also to carry the supplies necessary to keep the armies provisioned when on campaign. The advent of steam trains and railways changed the emphasis away from muscle power of animals and placed it on mechanical power. At the end of the journey, soldiers would still have to disembark to march the last remaining miles and equipment and supplies would have to be offloaded often some distance from its final destination. Horses were also transported by rail to be delivered fresh and ready for duty.

Military thinkers of the day understood the importance of horses on the battlefield and the roles in which they operated. They had come to terms with trains and realised their importance. One of these was Helmuth Von Moltke. Born in 1800, he served in the Prussian army from 1821, and died in 1891. During his long and varied military career he had witnessed many innovations, one of which was the introduction of the steam train. He recognised the importance the railway would have on military planning and whilst serving on the General Staff he remarked that Germany should 'Build no more fortresses, build railways.' Among the many other changes he may have seen, or at least heard about, was the development of the bicycle and the first military experiments in their use. Had he lived he would almost certainly have been among those who realised its military importance and advocated its introduction in service within the army.

Another military planner of the day was Alfred von Schlieffen, who served as head of the German General Staff from 1897 until 1906. It was on his plans that the German army would base its strategy in the opening stages of the First World War in August 1914. Schlieffen served in the Prussian army from 1821 and saw active serve in the Austro-Prussian War of 1866 and the Franco-Prussian War of 1870–71. He agreed with von Moltke in assessing the importance railways would have in time of war and instructed officers that they 'Don't just count an enemy's battalions; what is the extent of his railways?' Schlieffen died in 1913 and did not see the fruits of his labour put into practice and exactly what part, if any, he believed bicycles could play in his plans is not revealed.

General Douglas Haig, commander of the British Expeditionary Force on the Western Front in Belgium and France from 1915 to 1918, still believed strongly in the role of horses on the battlefield. Before the outbreak of war he had written: 'The role of the cavalry on the battlefield will always go on increasing... the organization and training of cavalry must have as its basis the necessity of mass tactics.' After the battle of Neuve Chapelle in March 1915, when it became obvious to most that the days of the cavalry on the battlefield were over, Haig persisted in his belief in the supremacy of the cavalry. In an analysis published in October 1918 concerning the action at Reumont, west of La Cateau, involving the Canadian Cavalry Brigade, the conclusion reached was that, while it had been successful, 'The cavalry had done nothing that the infantry, with artillery support and cyclists, could not have done for itself at less cost.'

Use of the motorcar was spreading but the mechanical unreliability of the early designs caused the military to treat them with scepticism. The bicycle, on the other hand, was a different matter. Being a machine, it did not require food or water like a horse, and not being motorised it did not require fuel either. Military theorists were quick to point out that when troops rode them into action, bicycles could be left in a central location without any need to be looked after like horses. Some observed that soldiers on bicycles had a smaller profile than cavalry and would therefore be less noticeable; they could seek cover behind trees and bushes and be more difficult to hit. They further argued that large numbers of horses make a lot of noise when on the move and create clouds of dust in dry weather. Others, however, pointed out that a typical battalion of infantry, around one thousand men, all riding bicycles, would also make noise and kick up plenty of dust.

Cavalry always resists any attempt to take away their horses and the suggestion of being replaced by a man on a bicycle would have been preposterous to men such as General Haig. To them, a man on a horse was the best weapon on the battlefield. But modern wars, such as the Russo-Japanese War of 1904–5, were proving how massed rifle fire, modern artillery and machine guns, could stop cavalry in its tracks.

Also during the Russo-Japanese War, bicycles were used by Russian Gendarmerie troops, who conducted patrols along the Trans-Siberian railway riding specially adapted bicycles fitted with stabilising wheels known as 'outrigger' wheels which fitted on the opposite rail. This was just as fast as a man on a horse and much faster than foot patrols. The British army had used bicycles during the Boer War in South Africa between 1899 and 1902 in this same role.

But for the time being the future of the horse was secure. There was no way in which the bicycle could ever be considered the equal of a horse in terms of versatility or agility; a man on a bicycle cannot pull a wagon or ride up rugged mountain routes to scout. They certainly could not be ridden to form a charge like cavalry either, with drawn swords held out at arm's length or lances tucked couched-fashion under the arm as in the Charge of the Light Brigade. But to provide the means to move hundreds or even thousands of troops quickly and independently, the bicycle was unquestionably the easiest solution. It took time to train a man to ride a horse, but basic skills in riding a bicycle can be mastered in a couple of hours, and a bicycle could be purchased for a fraction of the price of a horse. War would reveal the limitations of the bicycle as it did those of the horse, but that did not prevent either of them being used by the armies of the day. In fact both were used, serving alongside one another.

To ordinary soldiers the sight of so many men riding bicycles with their tubular frames which looked like something conjured up by a plumber caused some amusement and led to various nicknames, the one most widely used by the British army being 'the gaspipe cavalry'.

Some believed that in riding a bicycle the men would not develop sore feet on the march. Indeed they expounded the belief that in riding a bicycle a soldier's fitness would increase, thereby allowing him to remain in action for longer.

In South Africa in 1900 bicycles were sometimes found to be more useful than horses. British forces around Pretoria were being attacked by coordinated Boer forces and reinforcements were desperately required. Artillery was brought forward supported by five companies of infantry to join in the area known as the Nek. An officer was dispatched on horseback to take a message to Pretoria which would explain the situation to Lord Roberts and Lord Kitchener. After riding ten miles into his journey the officer encountered a civilian riding a bicycle. He decided this would be a better form of transportation and swapped his horse for the machine and instructed the man to await his return. Arriving in Pretoria he gave an appraisal of the situation at the Nek and reinforcements were sent. The officer, having rested, started on his return journey riding the borrowed bicycle. Unfortunately, the account does not state if he retrieved his horse and returned the bicycle to the owner, but this episode does demonstrate that the bicycle was at least a valuable replacement for a tired horse on that occasion, and probably saved lives.

In 1905, the same year as Russia and Japan were engaged in a fierce war, the Swiss army accepted into service bicycles known as the 'Ordonnanz Fahrrad Modell-05' or MO-05. Switzerland had a history of armed neutrality, a stance it had established in 1815. That position, however, did not prevent it from having a standing army for the defence of the country. Bicycles gave mobility to the troops in this small country. The basic MO-05 design weighed 52 pounds and was fitted with wheels with a diameter of 26 inches. The height of the handlebars and saddle could be adjusted to suit all sizes. Built by factories such as Condor, Cosmos, Casar and Schwalbe, the bicycles had various attachment points on the frame to allow document and map cases and personal weapons. Medics could carry supplies in panniers strapped to the frames. For repair and maintenance in the field, each bicycle carried a tool kit and puncture repair kit. For the next 100 years the Swiss army would continue to use the bicycle as a mode of transport, upgrading to new designs along the way.

Chapter 2

Armies find their Wheels 1888–1914

By 1887 the British army had become sufficiently curious about the bicycle to conduct a series of military exercises with the intention of testing the ability to move large numbers of troops quickly and effectively over long distances. It was proposed that the movement be done at the same time as horses and infantry marching on foot in its time-honoured fashion. Railway was not included as by this time mass transportation of troops by railway was already well proven from actual results achieved in wartime conditions during conflicts such as the American Civil War of 1861–65, the Austro-Prussian War of 1866 and the Franco-Prussian War of 1870–71.

The British army had already conducted earlier exercises in Kent in 1885 and 1886 and were keenly watching developments happening across Europe. The Italian army probably began the trend when it used bicycles in exercises conducted at Somma in 1875, during which riders covered twelve miles in an hour to deliver messages between the general staff and battalion commanders. By 1886 the Italian army had established companies of infantry equipped with bicycles in every regiment and in 1905 the Milan-based company of Edoardo Bianchi, which had been established in 1885 for the production of bicycles, produced its first bicycle specifically designed for the Italian army. Known as the Modello Militaire Brevettato or 'Model 1912' it was a folding style based on a civilian design. Some 45,000 were produced each year. Bianchi also supplied machines to Russia, where the factory of Leitner copied the design and produced them for the Russian army as the 'Dux Battle' fitted with brackets to carry weapons and other equipment. The factory of Leitner had been founded by Alexander Leitner (sometimes written as Leutner) in 1880 and based in Riga. It was the largest bicycle manufacturing factory in Russia and, fearing it would be captured by the Germans during the First World War, it was relocated to the Ukraine.

Between 1885 and 1886 the Austrian army staged a series of military exercises with riders on bicycles being used as messengers. At one point a fully equipped unit of infantry rode for five days, covering sixty miles a day on some days. Another unit exceeded that distance by riding an impressive 100 miles in one day. One of the leading bicycle manufacturers in Austria was the company of Puch, which in the mid-1890s was producing around 6,000 machines annually. By 1912 this figure had increased to 16,000, and throughout the First World War the company would supply bicycles to the Austrian army. Looking at what Italy, Austria and Britain were achieving, the German army in 1886 began using bicycles to deliver messages between Konigsberg, Strasbourg, Cologne and Posen.

The French army was also using bicycles, being actively encouraged to do so by General August Victor Cornat, commanding XVIII Corps. In 1886 he was 60 years old and had fought in Algeria, the Crimean War, Mexico in 1859, and in the Franco-Prussian War of 1870–71 where he distinguished himself at the Battle of St Privat. He was probably aware of developments in the use of bicycles in other armies and may have heard some of the presentations on their potential use by the military. During large-scale exercises in 1886, cyclists were delivering messages between garrisons along France's border with Germany. It was remarked by senior officers that the riders, even after several hours, were still quite fresh. General Cornat reported that during the exercises no horses had been used as messengers and cyclists had delivered all correspondence. A special bulletin was issued which offered inducements, such as better pay, to encourage reservists to parade using their own machine. The appeal worked, but selection was strict and only the very best men were accepted.

In America, Brevet Lieutenant Colonel Albert Augustus Pope established his own company in 1878 to produce the 'Columbia' brand, having started by importing bicycles from England. Pope had served in the Union army during the American Civil War, seeing fighting at the Battle of Antietam on 17 September 1862. He became interested in bicycles following a visit by a friend from England who encouraged him to become involved. In 1887, Pope stated that he believed the number of cyclists in Britain to be around 350,000 while in America that figure was around 50,000. How he arrived at these figures is unclear, but by 1890 his company was producing 250,000 bicycles a year. It then diversified into the manufacture of motor vehicles.

In a move designed to bring his bicycles to the attention of the American military, Pope, being the shrewd businessman he was, sent examples of his machines to militia units for trials. In 1892 he published a book called *Cycle Infantry Drill*, using the 'Soldier's Standard Bicycle', this being the military version of his civilian 'Columbia Light Roadster' design, to illustrate the work. The Chicago Exposition of 1893 was ideally suited to showcase his machines, both military and civilian designs. He was acquainted with Major General Nelson Miles, who had served as a Lieutenant Colonel in the 61st New York Volunteer Infantry Regiment during the American Civil War; they both fought at the Battle of Antietam. Using his connections, he tried to convince Miles of the value of bicycles to the military. But despite all his hard work and self-promotion, Pope did not secure any military contracts for his company.

The British army exercises of 1887 were so successful it was decided to repeat them the following year. This time, however, while not a complete disaster, the exercise of 1888 was not the success of the previous year. The results were mixed and, depending on one's point of view, were neither conclusive nor inconclusive on the future military use of the bicycle. Several designs had been used, including tricycles and machines which were pedalled by multiple riders. Some proved stable but were not well suited to uneven terrain. Tricycles were considered as potential platforms on which to mount the new machine guns to provide mobility, and the larger designs showed the potential to transport equipment and ammunition. One outstanding failure was a machine operated by three men from the 26th Middlesex Regiment which was being used to tow a Maxim machine gun. It was too heavy and had to be abandoned altogether. Nevertheless, the British Army was inclined to reserve judgement and give the bicycle and its new variants the benefit of the doubt; the exercises had once again demonstrated the feasibility of moving troops and in that respect the manoeuvres were successful.

One observer of the exercises was Lieutenant Colonel A.R. Savile of the Royal Irish Regiment, who at the time was serving as Professor of Tactics at the Royal Military College. He presented a paper to the Royal United Services Institution in London in which he expressed his opinion that the bicycle had proved that it had 'the power to transport infantry rapidly from point to point in a theatre of war… one of the most urgent requirements of modern warfare.' One design he dismissed was the 'Penny-Farthing', perhaps unsurprisingly due to its high centre of gravity and its height which precluded it from transporting supplies.

Savile was commanding officer of the Volunteer Cyclists at the time of the exercises of 1887 and 1888. He was also serving as the president of the War Office Committee appointed to report on the training and equipment for bicycle troops and, as such, it could be argued, Savile had a vested interest in proving his case. After all, as an expert on military cycling, it would be his recommendation which would lead to the choice of bicycle used by the army.

Savile drew up his report, in which he balanced both sides of the argument concerning the future use of bicycles in the army. He began by considering the options of bicycle designs available. Firstly there was the 'ordinary bicycle', which he discounted on handling characteristics and on the lack of ease with which the rider could mount and dismount. Secondly was the 'safety-bicycle', featuring rear driving safety, better handling, and speed and rider control, especially when descending steep gradients. It was sufficiently robust to carry the kit of the soldier riding, and it was easy to transport by train or ship when the army was deployed overseas allowing it to go into use immediately on arrival at its destination. Savile suggested that if the army standardised on a single design it would allow interchangeability of parts for repairs.

The other three styles of bicycle he considered useful were: the single tricycle, which he believed could be used to transport supplies and ammunition; the so-called 'tandem-bicycle' which could be ridden by two men. This could be used for similar purposes and had extra capacity to transport supplies if ridden by only one man; and the 'multi-cycle' design, such as the 'quadricycle' with four wheels to give a stable platform and operated by two men, which could provide transport for the evacuation of wounded men. He dismissed the 'novelty' designs, such as those with pairs of wheels mounted side by side, as being unsuitable for any military use.

Savile's paper would lead to the formation of one of the first cyclist regiments, the 26th Middlesex (Cyclist) Volunteer Corps, which had taken part in the movement exercises of 1888 and had originally comprised three companies, 'A', 'B' and 'C', attached to the King's Royal Rifle Corps. They had been joined in the cyclist exercises of the Bristol Engineer Corps and others from the 28th Middlesex. Before the end of the year several other Volunteer cyclist corps had been established, one of which was the 20th Middlesex Volunteers, which had been raised in 1860 and by 1897 had 828 cyclists of all ranks. Despite these specialist creations, it would not be for another twenty years, in 1908, when, as part of the Army Reforms initiated by the Secretary of State for War, Lord Haldane, that the unit would become a Territorial Force battalion as part of the newly created London Regiment. Bicycles were purchased from Singer & Company of Coventry, but progress to introduce the bicycle into the army was still slow. At this time a training scheme was set up, supervised by Major G.M. Fox, the Assistant Inspector of Gymnasia at Aldershot.

It was becoming increasingly realised that the roles of messenger or reconnaissance could often be performed just as well by a man on a bicycle as on a horse. It was not always the case: for example, where roads were impassable due to flooding or erosion a man on foot or horse-mounted was better. There was still scepticism. To truly prove their value, they would have to be put to the test in a real war situation. That test was to come soon.

Three years after the British army had concluded its trials with bicycles the American army began to investigate the potential use of bicycles in military roles. In 1891 the First Signal Corps of the Connecticut National Guard was chosen to raise the first military bicycle unit in the American army. Soldiers were detailed as riders to deliver messengers. In one demonstration, a rider delivered a message in less time than it took the semaphore system using the flag signalling method. Trials over short distances were bound to succeed; but what was needed was a demonstration over distance. In one demonstration a relay team of riders covered nearly 800 miles between Chicago and New York City to deliver a message. They completed the task in 4 days and 13 hours, an average of 7.3 miles an hour, during which they experienced severe weather conditions. Another demonstration saw riders deliver a message from Washington, DC, to Denver in just over six days, a distance of 1,600 miles, an average of just over 11 miles an hour.

The US army conducted various trials in 1896, perhaps because of Major General Nelson Miles, who by now was Commanding General of the US Army – head of the army. He may have had time to reflect on the proposals made to him by Colonel Pope four years earlier and decided to give bicycles a chance. One set of trials involved Colonel Pope, who announced that his company's 'Columbia Model 40' bicycle was to be used as a platform on which to mount a Colt machine gun, the weapon being fitted to the handlebars. The air-cooled weapon known as the M1895, weighing 35 pounds and firing 450 rounds per minute, was already in service with the US Navy. Being three feet five inches long and rather heavy it had to be mounted on a pedestal for firing, which on a warship was not a problem. The bicycle provided a solution.

A special bracket was developed to provide the weapon with traverse to allow the rider to engage targets. When not in use, the gun was strapped to the crossbar of the frame. The main drawback to its use in battle would have been the weight exerted on the front wheel of the bicycle. When firing, this increased and the wheel could sink into the ground. Other practicalities, such as loading the weapon and keeping it supplied with ammunition, and its great height mounted on handlebars of a bicycle further excluded it from such use. Trials with the combination did not impress the army and nothing came from the exercise. It was not an auspicious start and men such as Pope could only hope that Lt Moss's plans would be more successful. The Colt M1895 came in several calibres and was used by several overseas armies, including Britain and Russia, but the combination of it being mounted to fire from a bicycle was never used and no army adopted the design.

Machine guns were best being operated from a ground emplaced platform such as a tripod; bicycles with two wheels did not make the most stable mounting from which to fire. If machine guns were to be mounted on bicycles it would have to be on either tricycle or quadricycle designs, which by the 1890s had all but been ruled out from military service. In Britain in 1896, the weapon inventor Hiram Percy Maxim, son of the late Hiram Maxim who had designed a machine gun, also arranged for a trial using the Colt machine gun mounted on a tricycle, the difference being that Maxim arranged for it to be mounted over the rear axle of a tandem tricycle built by Rudge-Whitworth. But even when pedalled by two men the weight of the combination was too heavy to negotiate even slight inclines; the results of experiments conducted ten years earlier were confirmed.

End-of-century conflicts such as the Spanish-American War and the Sudan War of 1881–99 showed such designs to be the military anachronisms they were. But this did not prevent the idea of machine guns on bicycles from being considered from time to time. Indeed right up until 1916 the French army was conducting trials of such designs using bicycles in the middle of the First World War. The idea was only able to become successful with the motorcycle and sidecar combination, which provided mobility and a stable firing platform capable of carrying its own ammunition supply. These types of machines would be used during both world wars, with some armies still using such designs in the 1990s.

Meanwhile, Lieutenant James A. Moss, a keen cyclist, continued to promote the bicycle, with bicycles for the troops being supplied by the Spalding Bicycle Company of Springfield, Massachusetts. In 1896, at Fort Missoula in Montana, Lieutenant Moss began planning a demonstration using forty black soldiers from the 25th Infantry Regiment. Moss proposed his 'Cycle Corps' ride to St. Louis, Missouri, covering more than 1,900 miles, making it the most gruelling undertaking to date. The exercise was expected to last six weeks, during which each man would ride his bicycle, weighing 55 pounds, for up to 10 hours to cover 40 miles a day. Each man carried rations for two days, his knapsack, blanket roll and shelter half tent, along with his rifle and 50 rounds of ammunition. Much of the route planned by Moss ran parallel with the railway line which allowed him to arrange for resupply points every 100 miles along the route. The soldiers had trained with their bicycles before the exercise, but even so it would be a test of endurance with the route taking the soldiers across hostile terrain and expose them to extreme weather conditions.

The exercise began on 14 June 1897 with the small group cycling out of the barracks. There were times when stages of the route reached heights of 5,000 feet and the machines had to be pushed by the dismounted riders. It was physically demanding work for the 'wheelmen' as they became known. They were accompanied by a journalist called Edward Boos who wrote a series of features on the group's progress for the *Daily Missoulian* newspaper. Readers who were also cyclists were curious enough to ride out to see the soldiers pass. The exercise was completed by the entire group on 24 July within the specified time – not one man dropped out. It was a success and showed that even when faced with unexpected hazards such as bad roads or natural obstacles such as rivers, the riders could improvise solutions and continue their journey. Except for the shooting, it was the closest thing to actual combat conditions. To put it into context, the black soldiers had cycled almost twice the distance covered by Napoleon's army in 1812 when it marched to Moscow.

Lieutenant Moss wrote a report on the exercise in which he outlined the value of the bicycle for reconnaissance duties, the sending of messages and even traffic control. He stressed that troops using bicycles as independent transport could be used as a mobile reserve force rather than committing them as static frontline troops. That way, he believed, they could secure positions such as bridges or strongpoints until reinforcements arrived. He did accept that in wet conditions and ruinous roads the horse was superior and it would be ridiculous to think the bicycle could supplant the horse. The exercises involving the First Signals Corps had been useful but did not stretch the physical endurance of the soldiers. Moss's exercise was more realistic. The bicycle would suit men from the cities who had no horse skills but would probably have known how to ride a bicycle. He concluded that horses and bicycles be used together. It was an obvious summing up already being reached in other armies, including Britain and France.

Despite the success, nothing further was done to establish a regular Bicycle Corps and, no doubt very frustratingly for Lieutenant Moss after all his hard work, the unit reverted to its regular role as infantry. The men from Moss's exercise went on to take part in some of the heaviest fighting during the Spanish-American War of 1898 including the attack against San Juan Hill on Cuba.

Moss and Pope, who were delighted with the promising results, must have been disappointed when General Nelson Miles did not create a bicycle force. He retired in 1903 and still the US Army did not pursue the formation of cyclist units. It would not be until twenty years after Moss's trial that the US Army issued bicycles to troops when America went to war in 1917. Even then, no specific role for bicycle troops was identified or developed.

By the end of the nineteenth century the bicycle was firmly established in civilian society if not yet within the military. Bicycles had been used in limited roles by the military, but that was during peacetime military exercises. Now the British army was about to show how useful they could be in war when troops were sent to South Africa in 1899 with the outbreak of the Second Boer War. The almost three-year long war, in which battalions of the Regular British Army and Colonial forces from Australia fought against an armed group of farmers, proved to be one of the British Empire's bloodiest conflicts.

The only means of traversing the vast wilderness of South Africa were either horseback, or the railway network which extended hundreds of miles between the major settlements. The British army controlled the railway and used it to transport troops and supplies. This led to the Boers targeting the routes and destroying the tracks using explosives. The British army countered this by using patrols mounted on horses to protect the lines. They also developed a hand-operated trolley called a 'draisine' powered by two men using a pump action on handles. Virtually silent, it was useful to scout ahead for danger and could be used to cover miles of track.

The British army was still wearing brightly-coloured scarlet tunics as part of the uniform during the early stages of the Boer War, as seen here with the Lancashire Fusiliers.

An alternative solution based on the Draisine design was the use of bicycle-style pedals to operate the trolley. Other variations appeared, including a pair of bicycle frames connected side by side fitted with wheels suitable for use on the tracks. The two men could carry their equipment, supplies and weapons with them on their patrol. Any attempt to use standard bicycles in open territory was severely hampered by the poor conditions of the compacted dry earth road network, which, while passable in the dry season, became unusable during the wet. This limited any bicycle use to short distances and only during dry conditions when the roads were hard. Boer units did on occasion use bicycles in a more ambitious manner, such as the 'Theron se Verkenningkorps' (Theron Reconnaissance Patrol), named after its founder, Daniel Theron, a Boer commander. The British offered a huge reward for the capture of Theron 'dead or alive'. Despite these partially successful attempts to employ bicycles, both sides found that it was the versatile horse which proved to be the best means of mobility in these harsh conditions. Certainly the Boer farmers would have felt more comfortable riding a horse than trying to pedal a bicycle.

Among the British regiments deployed to South Africa was the Lancashire Fusiliers, which took some bicycles with them for delivering messages. In November 1899, Major General Sir Edward Yewd Brabant raised a unit of Light Horse known as 'Brabant's Horse'. It comprised volunteers from Britain, South Africa and Australia and had a complement of around 600 men. Among its duties, the unit conducted operations against the Boers and, although mounted on horses, some troops serving as messengers rode bicycles. It was a short-lived unit, being disbanded in December 1901. In the end, it was the practicality of the horse in the extremes of terrain which won through.

In March, 1899, several months before the outbreak of the Boer War, Major Baden Fletcher Smyth Baden-Powell, who had seen extensive campaign service in the Middle East, including the Sudan, presented a paper to the Royal United Services Institution on the subject of military cycling to the Royal United Services Institution, entitled 'The Bicycle for War Purposes'. In it he suggested that a regular training programme to familiarise troops with bicycles be introduced at the army's main base at Aldershot in Hampshire. He continued by stating that it was an opportune moment for the army to reach a decision concerning 'the exact pattern of machine most suitable for military purposes'. Baden-Powell was not just a theorist when it came to bicycles. He was also a designer and in 1901 developed his own idea for a collapsible machine known as the 'Tripartite'. It was based on the standard safety bicycle but featuring certain modifications which he designed, such as the forks, front wheel, steering post, and handlebar which could be removed from the frame for ease of stowage during transportation on trains or horse-drawn wagons. It took less time to prepare his machine for action than it did for other designs of folding bicycle. Furthermore, the frame of the Tripartite remained assembled when collapsed yet still made for a compact cargo load for stowage.

In his presentation Baden-Powell outlined the conditions which might see the judicious use of bicycles by the army. Firstly, there was the use by troops on home service during an emergency to counter an invasion, for which he suggested a lightweight machine for quick response. The roads across Britain were generally of good quality which meant fast movement and limited mechanical failure. Secondly, he covered those overseas countries which also had roads of good quality. For these he suggested a sturdy design capable of carrying loads. Lastly he focused on overseas deployments where roads were lacking or of poor quality, exactly the type which troops would encounter on campaign in South Africa. For this he suggested a heavy-framed machine with stout wheels, capable of withstanding heavy wear and tear.

Once Baden-Powell had established that different circumstances required different designs of machines, he went on to outline several roles in which bicycles might be used. Firstly, bicycles could be used for the strategic movement of large numbers of troops to specified destinations without the need for railways. Secondly, bicycles could be used by troops to move fast into enemy-held territory to destroy a specific target such as a bridge or to sever communications. The idea of using riders on bicycles for scouting and reconnaissance was familiar, but Baden-Powell expanded on the idea by suggesting they could be used as either rear or advance guards.

The suggestion of using them as mounted infantry, in much the same way that regiments of dragoons had been used, was another idea which had been widely considered. Baden-Powell broadened the concept by expanding the role of cyclist infantry to include them as part of an all-arms force, which would include providing escorts to convoys, artillery trains and supply columns. When undertaking these duties, they would be expected to fight as infantry to protect their charges from enemy attack. The role of men on bicycles serving as orderlies and messengers made perfect sense and was already a proven duty. Next was the possible use of the bicycles to provide troops with their own independent means of transport. This function had long been recognised but Baden-Powell expanded on it suggesting that bicycles could be used to bring supplies forward and in doing so help ease the burden on logistics lines. Once they had delivered their cargo, the bicycles could be used to help evacuate lightly wounded troops to base hospitals.

Lastly, he looked at some more specialist roles in which bicycles might prove useful. There was no reason why a man trained in telegraphy or some other form of signalling, such as semaphore or heliography, for communicating over long distances, should not ride a bicycle to widen the scope of these roles and give mobility on the battlefield. The signaller could be accompanied by an armed escort who could also carry equipment and, when needed, they could establish a base from where to transmit messages or pass on information concerning enemy movements, after which the small group could rejoin the main body. What Baden-Powell was suggesting was nothing new, because traditional horsed cavalry was already performing these duties; it was his idea to use bicycles in these roles which was different.

At first it appeared that he was suggesting the army would need different designs to suit each role. The question was: 'Why have so many different machines to complete these tasks, when the cavalry only requires one horse to complete the same duties?' He replied that all he was suggesting was that each man be issued with a bicycle according to his size. He pointed out that in the cavalry horses were ridden by men suitable to the size of the mount; why should it not be the same for bicycles? He concluded by pointing out that the army only required a design of bicycle which was sturdy, could be easily maintained and repaired by the rider using tools and spare parts carried on the bicycle. By keeping the design simple it would reduce the chance of mechanical failure. A standardised design would allow for the interchangeability of parts. For example, a universal-sized wheel would allow the same tyres to be used on any machine.

Baden-Powell had presented a well thought out case for the use of bicycles within the army, but he did not recommend any particular manufacturer. He mentioned folding or collapsible bicycles because of their compactness for storage and transport, but when it came to the final decision as to which design would be best for service, that choice could only be made by the War Department which was responsible for supplying the army with equipment.

The choice was made two years later in 1901, when the British army introduced its first official service machine known as the 'Bicycle (Mark I) High, Medium, Low'. Manufactured by BSA, it was one design in three categories of size to suit soldiers of different sizes. After all, uniforms from boots to head-dress were in different sizes to fit soldiers and the same applied to bicycles. Each machine had attachments including bell, lamp, pump and pump-clips, and cycle rest. Carriers were fitted to the front and rear so riders could carry equipment such as blankets and tents. Rifle clips were fitted to the frame so that the rider did not have to operate the bicycle with his weapon slung across his back. Also, as Baden-Powell had suggested, each machine carried a tool kit in a bag containing spanners and oil.

In 1902 the British army introduced the Mark II Bicycle into service, which incorporated several design changes, including free-wheel hub. Six years later, in 1908, the Mark III Bicycle, with further modifications, including coaster hub with free wheel clutch and changes to the frame and front forks, entered service. It must have been gratifying for men such as Savile and Baden-Powell to see their suggestions being implemented, including the standardisation of models. Other armies across Europe were beginning to follow suit, but it was the British army which led the way in the use of bicycles in the military. This lead was maintained with the introduction of the Mark IV Bicycle in 1911, which came in the one standard size frame of 24 inches.

This design replaced the need for two additional sized frames, and the shape of the 'flat' or parallel handlebars was changed to a style which was slightly turned up. The Mark I to Mark IV Bicycles were all produced by BSA, but other British companies manufacturing bicycles, such as Rudge

By the end of the Boer War the British army had adopted the khaki uniform, as seen being worn by Brabant's Horse and a dispatch rider of the Duke of Edinburgh's Volunteer Rifles.

and Royal Enfield, also produced bicycles for the army. The Enfield Cycle Company in Redditch, Worcestershire, had its origins in light industry when George Townsend established the company in 1851. In 1882 his son, also George, began manufacturing components for bicycles, but the company ran into difficulties. In 1891 the company failed and underwent a series of changes of name before emerging as the Enfield Autocar. The change of fortune was partly due to Robert Walker Smith who had been an engineer at the bicycle manufacturing company of Rudge in Coventry. In the following years further companies also produced bicycles for the British army and overseas forces, including Raleigh, Sunbeam and Whitworth.

One person who did not share the opinion that bicycles had a role in warfare was the British General Sir Redvers Buller, who had been awarded the Victoria Cross for his bravery at the Battle of Hlobane in the Zulu War of 1879. In 1899, when the Second Boer War broke out, he was given command of the Natal Field Force in South Africa, but his poor performance at engagements such as the battles of Colenso, Magersfontein and Stormberg, led to him being relieved of his command. Buller's less than able handling of a field command gained him many critics, one of whom was Viscount Esher, who described him as 'a gallant fellow but no strategist'. In his service life Buller had witnessed many changes in the army and the introduction of innovations, but, in his opinion, he could not see any practical use of the bicycle by the military.

Chapter 3

Tyre Treads 1914–18

As the nineteenth century closed, the industrial might which would propel Germany to become the powerhouse of Europe was growing at a phenomenal rate. The German army exploited this to put it on course to become one of the most powerful military forces in Europe. Included in this was bicycles, with which the army conducted trials, using models produced by companies such as Adler, Gritzner and Kayser. Another bicycle manufacturing company was Durkopp, which in 1861 had begun as a manufacturer of sewing machines but by 1889 was established as one of the leading manufacturers of bicycles. In 1905 it was supplying machines to the German army, such as the Herrenrad Victoria 'Model 12' with a 24-inch frame and 28-inch wheels, the same sizes used by the British army. The machines were modified to military use by fitting attachments to carry the rider's weapon and secure dispatch containers for messengers carrying orders and other documents.

The German army created specialist bicycle units known as 'Radfahr Kompanies' and 'Radfahr Battaillonen' organised to be at the strength of one Company per Jäger Battalion. By 1896 the German army was conducting extended military exercises involving the use of bicycles with riders covering routes of up to 100 miles. What had started as a series of exercises ten years earlier, with messengers delivering orders and communications, was now being taken seriously. By 1914 there would be eighty cycle companies in the German army. Gritzner would continue as one of the leading suppliers of military bicycles and in 1918 alone the company produced 30,000 machines of the more than 125,000 bicycles issued for use by the German army during the war.

In France the role of bicycles in war was also being considered. Even the historically neutral states, such as Holland, neutral since 1830, Belgium, Switzerland and Sweden, were investigating how best to integrate the machines into their national armies. The Dutch army maintained a position

A German army parade with a bicycle in the foreground fitted with what appears to be a reel for laying cables for field telephones. It is also fitted with a box for either tools or carrying messages.

of armed neutrality with an army held at a strength of around 200,000 with a combination of horses and bicycles for mobility. Belgium also adopted a position of armed neutrality, having its army ready and trained in the event of an attack. It had established units of military cyclists, which included four Carabinier battalions equipped with machines known as 'Belgica'. The troops in these units had undergone training at a regimental cyclist school where they received lessons in map reading, reconnaissance, reporting, carrying messages and basic field maintenance for the repair of their bicycles.

Portugal, Spain, Denmark and Serbia, were also showing interest in bicycles for their national armies.

The Germans attacked Belgium just after 8 am on the morning of 4 August 1914 as two divisions and two cavalry corps amounting to about 60,000 men crossed the border into Belgium at Gemmenich. Not meeting any opposition, they continued their advance. Just after 10 am they had passed Thimister-Clermont when a German scouting party mounted on bicycles encountered a small group of Belgian lancers approaching them. The Germans opened fire killing a young lancer, Antoine Adolphe Fonck

Bicycles had to be repaired by the riders under all conditions, even under artillery fire.

of the 1st Squadron of the 2nd Lancers Regiment. The Belgian army had sustained its first casualty of the war, inflicted by a German army cyclist. Five hours later the Germans had reached the Meuse river, which had been their object on that first day of their 'Handstreich' (sudden attack), with orders to capture the bridges across the waterway.

The force, while large, was but a tiny fragment of the German commitment to the attack by seven armies with a combined total of almost 1.5 million troops, marching westwards in a seemingly unstoppable advance. Amongst this great force were thirty-six independent companies of infantry mounted on bicycles, as well as a battalion of cyclists attached to each cavalry division with an additional ten reserve bicycle companies.

Germany would eventually mobilise around eleven million men, most of which served in the army on either the Western Front or, together with their Austro-Hungarian allies, facing the Russian army on the Eastern Front. In 1914 the German army had 669 battalions of infantry which by 1918 had increased to 2,300; it would expand to over 218 divisions. In 1914 there were 642 batteries of field artillery; four years later this had increased to 2,900. Between 1916 and 1918 the number of machine guns increased from 1,600 to 11,000.

Special machine gun companies, each with three troops equipped with two machine guns, were formed into cyclist battalions from 1916. These were deployed mainly on the Rumania Front. They comprised around fifty men, plus drivers for the vehicles and horse-drawn wagons used to transport the weapons, ammunition, stores and baggage. Each included at least one cyclist for liaison duties. Before the outbreak of war two Jäger battalions had cyclist troops formed into companies. By 1917 this structure had been increased to around 150 with companies being formed into cyclist battalions. By early 1917 three cyclist battalions were formed into a brigade that provided rearguard support during the withdrawal to the Hindenburg Line. Cyclist troops were also engaged in patrolling duties along the border between occupied Belgium and neighbouring neutral Holland to prevent messages being passed on to the Allies concerning movements by the German army.

Also on 4 August 1914 a column of the German advance was brought to a halt near the town of Visé, where it was frustrated to find the bridges over the Meuse had been destroyed by the Belgian 12th Infantry of the Line Regiment. As they were taking stock of the situation, the Germans observed a small group of gendarmes advancing towards them riding bicycles travelling from the direction of Gemmenich. The Germans opened fire killing two of the cyclists, Auguste Bouko and Jean-Pierre Thill. This was the second of the opening skirmishes on the first day of the war, both of which, albeit rather minor, had involved cyclist troops in some way. The actions clearly demonstrated that troops on bicycles would be involved in the fighting. Exactly how their value could be put to use on a larger scale would be demonstrated over the next few days. For seven days the Germans were forced to remain in their positions while the bridges were repaired. They used the time to conduct local scouting duties before moving forward to cross the river on 9 August.

In England, the first 80,000 men of the British Expeditionary Force, as promised by the British government would be sent to the aid of France and Belgium, were preparing to set off by train to their embarkation ports at Portsmouth and Southampton, bound for Boulogne, Le Havre and Rouen. It included 30,000 horses for the cavalry and artillery, 125 machine guns and 315 field guns. At the outbreak of war, the strength of the British army stood at just over 250,000 all ranks. Between 1914 and 1918 it expanded greatly. For example, at the begging of the war there were 6,000 signallers in the army but by 1918 there were some 70,000, while the Royal Army Medical Corps expanded from 90,000 in 1914 to some 13,000 officers and 154,000 other ranks by 1918. One new unit to be raised in accordance with Army Order 477, dated 7 November 1914, was the Army Cyclist Corps (ACC).

A typical infantry battalion in the British army in 1914 had approximately 1,000 men of all ranks. Three such battalions with their attached support troops would form a brigade and a division could include three or four brigades. The divisional train, which was responsible for moving all necessary equipment and supplies, used horse-drawn wagons for this purpose but also included up to thirty bicycles for miscellaneous duties, including the carrying of messages. The cavalry was formed along similar lines, but a cavalry division could have nearly 7,500 riding horses and almost 3,000 used for pulling wagons and as packs animals. The cavalry train alone had 79 riding horses and 664 draught horses, along with several motor vehicles and around 40 bicycles.

Among the first infantry units to arrive in France were the 3rd Infantry Brigade of the 1st Division and the 6th Infantry Brigade of the 6th Division, both of which formed part of I Corps. They included the 1st and 2nd Cyclist Companies respectively. The 9th Infantry Brigade of the 3rd Division and the 15th Infantry Brigade of the 5th Division, forming part of II Corps, included the 3rd and 5th Cyclist Companies. Likewise, III Corps, which included the 12th Infantry Brigade in 4th Division and 18th Infantry Brigade of the 6th Division, which arrived in France between 31 August and 10 September 1914 after the first engagements with German troops at Mons, included the 4th and 6th Cyclist Companies. The inclusion of cyclist companies shows the importance which the British army placed on the bicycle at this stage of the war.

It took weeks for the whole of the BEF to assemble. The bulk of the troops arrived in France between 12 and 17 August, after which the battalions had to be assembled as brigades and organised with equipment. There were six infantry divisions, a cavalry division along with artillery support, medical and other supporting branches to total over 130,000 men. They now faced another train journey to take them east across France and into Belgium. Some were lucky to travel in carriages with seats while others sat in wagons designed to transport either forty men or eight horses. When sufficiently close to their destination, the troops would leave the trains and march the last few miles to take up positions around the Belgian town of Mons, a coal mining area, where they expected to engage the enemy. The bicycles which had been transported by train were issued to the designated troops as they prepared to continue their journey. The process to move so many men and their equipment and deploy them into position took time, which was a precious commodity of which the British army had little.

British soldiers found it easy to become lost and this man is asking directions from a local, even though the men cannot understand one another.

One of the infantry battalions to be issued with its share of the 14,000 bicycles taken to France was the 4th Battalion Middlesex Regiment. One contingent sailed from Southampton with 1,300 bicycles but fewer than 1,000 motor vehicles.

These British cyclist troops are mixing with French locals during the early days of the war.

Another contingent, also sailing from Southampton, included over 200 bicycles and 1,200 horses. By 1918 the number of bicycles issued to the British army during the war would reach 150,000 machines, used in all theatres of the war. For example, looking ahead, when the XIV Corps, commanded by Lieutenant General the Earl of Cavan, was sent to Italy in November 1917 it included the 14th Cyclist Battalion. When XI Corps, commanded by Lieutenant General Sir Richard Haking, arrived in Italy to join XIV Corps in December 1917, as well as including artillery, signals and engineers, it also had the 11th Cyclist Battalion attached.

The squadrons of Royal Engineers deployed with the BEF included 33 bicycles in their field companies while the Signals Squadron had 34. Even the Royal Artillery was equipped with bicycles. One bicycle was allocated to a battery of 18-pounder field guns and one for a battery of 4.5-inch howitzers. At brigade level the average numbers of bicycles held on strength was five machines, the exception being the Royal Horse Artillery which held twelve machines.

On 12 August the first boats carrying the advance guard of the BEF arrived at Boulogne while to the south German General Georg von der Marwitz, with six regiments, including a mounted cavalry force of 4,000 from the 2nd and 4th Cavalry Divisions, received orders to move, breaking his enforced wait along the Meuse River. He was directed to conduct reconnaissance patrols in the area between the cities of Liège, Brussels and Antwerp. With the bridges now repaired, his first scouting groups were sent out early in the morning. It was not long before the first of them returned with the news that the bridge at Haelen over the river Gete, just south of Diest, was being defended by Belgian troops. These were men from a force of almost 3,000 troops under the command of General Léon de Witte who had orders to defend the area. The city of Diest was an important transport and communication junction for the road and rail network in the area and the waterway extending south. The area is overlooked by the Bokkenberg hill, over 200 feet in height, and is a landmark in an otherwise low-lying open plain of sweeping fields of farmland. Several farms dotted the area, with the Ijzerwinning farm becoming one of the most prominent points during the battle. The Belgians had already identified Haelen as the location most likely to be exploited by the advancing Germans and General de Witte had deployed his forces to the west of this location, extending between the villages of Liebroek, Velpen and Zelk. Included in this force was a unit of 450 cyclists from the Carabiniers Cyclistes Regiment, who would fight as dismounted infantry. Witte had some artillery to support his force which consisted mainly of cavalry. The Belgian troops used drainage ditches as defensive positions.

The first tentative contact between Belgian and German forces occurred around 8 am on the morning of 12 August and over the next four hours each side began to manoeuvre their troops into position. General de Witte had sent for reinforcements and was anxiously awaiting their arrival. At 1pm, the artillery of both sides opened fire. The Battle of Haelen had commenced. German infantry moved forward and although the bridge across the river had been blown up, it had not been destroyed completely. Enough of the structure remained to allow the Germans to cross the waterway, including mounted troops, and over 1,000 troops entered Haelen, driving out the 200 Belgian troops holding positions in the town. German cavalry advancing through the open fields were slowed down by the wire fences around the farms, making them prime targets for the Belgian machine gunners who took a heavy toll.

These Belgian troops, some on bicycles, are defending a bridge in the first weeks of the war in 1914.

Belgian reinforcements began to arrive which bolstered those troops who had been in action since early morning. Marwitz ordered his cavalry to advance and in response de Witte ordered a counter-attack with cavalry and dismounted cyclist troops fighting in the infantry role. Heavy fighting and artillery around the Ijzerwinning Farm led to the buildings being set on fire. By 4.30 pm, with both sides approaching exhaustion, Marwitz ordered his cavalry to withdraw towards Hasselt and Alken. They had mounted several charges which had been fought off and suffered heavy losses. De Witte's force was almost at a standstill, but it had given a good account of itself and held back a force more than twice its strength. It was determined to continue the fight, but the odds were stacked against it.

The battle at Haelen was a tactical victory for the Belgian army, in which cyclist troops, despite their few numbers, had played a significant part as trained riflemen. What they achieved was beyond expectations for an untried force; their efforts had contributed to forcing a temporary halt on the Germans. The Carabinier Cyclistes had made up twenty per cent of de Witte's force. Unfortunately it was just a small localised victory and did nothing to prevent the inevitable as the weight of the German army continued to press home its advance into Belgium and elsewhere.

Belgian losses amounted to around 160 killed and 320 men wounded. De Witte's small force had killed 150 Germans, wounded 600 and taken 300 prisoners. The Germans had also lost nearly 1,000 horses either killed or wounded. It became known as 'The battle of the Silver Helmets' because of the number of highly polished, silver cavalry helmets scattered across the fields during the fighting.

The 2nd Regiment of Carabinier Cyclists, known in Dutch as the 2nd Regiment Carabinier Wielrijders, had been formed in 1890 as an infantry regiment of riflemen in the Belgian army. By 1898 it had expanded to a complement of four full companies. In 1911 these companies were formed into a battalion within the regiment. It was following the Battle of Haelen that the battalion was given the nickname of 'Schwarze Teufel' or 'Black Devils' by the Germans who had faced them out of respect for the bravery of the Belgian soldiers. Following their success at Haelen, three more companies of cyclist troops were created, one each month in August, September and October, using reserve troops as they were called up. These became the 2nd Battalion in January 1915 and the original 2nd Battalion was given the new title of 1st Battalion and attached to the First Cavalry Division. By the end of the war in 1918, the 2nd Battalion Carabinier Cyclist was formed into the First Cavalry Division.

The German advance continued unabated, Antwerp was besieged in September and in October German troops entered the Belgian capital of Brussels. Other towns and cities fell, including Liège and Namur, forcing the Belgian army to withdraw westwards. In October Belgian troops were taking up defensive positions along the Yser Canal as it snaked northward towards the coast away from Diksmuide. To secure their defensive positions the Belgians opened the sluice gate of the Yser Canal allowing the sea to flood the area. It was a simple yet effective measure which stopped the Germans who had no choice but to adopt static positions.

There had been cyclist units in the Belgian army since 1898: one company in four in each infantry battalion was equipped with bicycles. Between 1911 and 1913 complete independent battalions of cyclist troops had been formed. With the coming of war things changed and in September each division in the Belgian army had either one or several cyclist companies. However, in a war that was becoming static left little scope was left for their use as mobile infantry.

Belgian troops served in other parts of the front line, but for the most part these defensive positions constituted the only option available to them. Bicycles produced by BSA in England were sent to replace those lost in the early months of the war. They were used for liaison purposes and other duties in the rear of the Belgian positions.

Two days after the battle of Haelen, on 14 August, 1,100 men of the 4th Battalion Middlesex Regiment landed at Boulogne-sur-Mer. In the next week they advanced 120 miles, sending ahead reconnaissance troops mounted on bicycles as it did so. Their duty was to report back anything they had observed. On 21 August they were approaching the town of Obourg. Two of the cyclists dispatched were Lance Corporal Beart and Private John Parr and it was they who first spotted German troops approaching. Parr dismounted and took cover in a ditch to keep watch on developments, Beart went back to report to the battalion. Unfortunately Parr was spotted and fatally wounded when the Germans opened fire. He was the first British soldier to be killed in the war and the first British soldier to be killed in a European war since the Battle of

The Belgian army held trenches along the Yser Canal which was unsuitable for bicycles.

Looking south along the Yser Canal where the Belgian trench line was static. Bicycles were used for liaison duties and delivering messages.

Waterloo in 1815. His age given on his enlistment papers was 20 but his birth certificate showed he was only 17.

The battalion, now alerted, did not allow the incident to distract it from its orders to deploy to designated positions and it continued forward to cross the border into Belgium, heading towards Bettignies, north of Mons on the Canal de Mons et Condé, where it was known that some roads in this area had already been captured by the Germans. The 4th Middlesex took up its positions on the south bank of the Canal de Mons et Condé, with the waterway acting like a defensive moat to the front, with the 4th Royal Fusiliers to their left, forming part of the 3rd Division around the town of Nimy. For the next two days the British troops waited, ready for the Germans they knew must come. On 23 August the waiting was over as the German artillery opened fire to support their infantry advance. Try as hard as they could the British positions could not hold. As the 12th Brandenburg Grenadiers approached the area of St Ghislain, they were engaged by the 1st Battalion Royal West Kents holding the area, which inflicted 500 casualties on them for only 100 killed and wounded in return.

The German determination to continue to advance would cost them dearly. With seven German armies totalling almost 1.5 million men, they outnumbered the combined forces of the British, French and Belgian Allies, who were now forced to conduct a fighting retreat. Communications were in disarray and the only way in which units could convey messages with any degree of reliability was by bicycle. The Germans found the most reliable means of conveying orders or information was to send *Meldegänger* or runners to carry messages by hand. Troops riding bicycles were serving in the important role of messengers, just as demonstrated in pre-war presentations.

The Allies tried to stabilise and contain the situation, but failed, and on 27 August the French and British armies resumed their retreat. For the next week the Allies fell back towards Paris, with some units covering more than 100 miles to escape the Germans. Equipment, weapons and other materiel was discarded along the route. The Germans had to move fast to remain in contact with the British and French armies. They had over-extended their lines of supply and were exhausted. Finally, the Allies halted at the River Marne and managed to stem the German advance,

The French army mobilised and marched to war with great confidence.

A column of French troops on the march, including bicycle troops.

before turning northwards and pushing towards the coast, trying to outflank the Germans.

In response, the Germans mirrored the move. This manoeuvring has come to be referred to as the 'Race to the Sea' as each side tried to outflank their opponent. Neither side achieved the upper hand and both sides arrived at the coast almost simultaneously. During this period, officers at all command levels used bicycle messengers to keep in contact with one another and to communicate with senior officers. Officers themselves also personally conveyed messages, such as Lieutenant the Honourable Lionel Tennyson of the 1st Rifle Brigade who in early September 1914 was serving as orderly officer attached to the headquarters of 11th Brigade of 4th Division. In the early hours of the morning 14 September, during the fighting retreat, he was awakened and told to report to Lieutenant Colonel L. Le Marchant, commanding officer of the 1st Battalion East Lancashire Regiment, which at the time was in the vicinity of the town of Ligny.

The battalion had landed in Le Havre on 22 August and been involved in some heavy fighting since then. Lieutenant Tennyson used a bicycle to deliver the message which ordered the East Lancashire Regiment to make ready to attack. He recalled how during his journey he was fired on by a German machine gun but managed to avoid being hit by using cover

A group of French Dragoons, mounted infantry, and some cyclist troops defending a railway line.

French cyclist troops with German prisoners of war.

to screen his movement. However, no sooner had Tennyson delivered his message than Lieutenant Colonel L. Le Marchant was shot and killed.

As the end of 1914 approached, with the onset of winter producing conditions which made it almost impossible to move, each side began to dig in. The network of trenches they dug would eventually extend from the Belgian coast to the Swiss border, almost 500 miles, and become known as the Western Front. At this stage in the war much of the road network system remained intact and passable by vehicles and bicycles. With this stagnation came the opportunity for armies to deploy their artillery which, over the next four years, would fire great barrages to prepare the way for offensives such as the Somme, Vimy Ridge, Messines and Passchendaele. The shells, fired in their millions, also smashed the roads.

Simply to move men along these shattered routes leading to the front line was an effort and to move heavy loads of supplies became a Herculean task. Men and horses waded through seas of mud and vehicles had to be manhandled through the great morass. The mud was so deep in places that men and horses drowned in it, and frequently vehicles had to be abandoned. The use of bicycles in such conditions was rendered virtually impossible, but that did not stop them from being held in reserve ready for use should the need or opportunity arise. Messengers or runners were used to deliver communications and these men had to leave the relative safety of the trenches to negotiate the battlefield which exposed them to enemy fire. They most often completed the task on foot, but just occasionally conditions did permit the use of bicycles. 'Duckboards' made of planks were laid out to help ease passage, and 'corduroy roads' were constructed of branches and planks for heavier vehicles; both could be used by cyclist messengers. Snow and ice could also severely hamper the use of bicycles. The frozen ground might have been hard, but a slippery surface would prevent the rider from obtaining traction. This would be even worse if tyres were worn or punctured.

One British soldier who found himself designated as a runner almost from the time he arrived in France in July 1915 was Private Robert Cude, who served with the 7th Battalion, The Buffs (East Kent) Regiment, part of 18th Division. He kept a diary of his time in the army until 1919. Cude was serving in the area of the Somme as final preparations were being made for the massive offensive due to begin on 1 July 1916. He recorded: 'I have had to push my cycle, in company with other "Runners", over roads three-inches deep in mud! Arrive midnight and drop to sleep straight away, awaking 7.30 am feeling completely washed out, for am

A mixed column of transport which includes trucks, motorcycles and bicycles.

Cyclist messengers could use the wooden duckboards as roadways to avoid the mud.

soaked to the skin. It is all in a day's march however, and we are on "Active Service", so must grumble but carry on.'

Robert Cude's willingness to 'carry on' despite the mud demonstrates his commitment to do his duty which would earn him the Military Medal and Bar for bravery. His writing describes how regardless of conditions he had to deliver messages and return with the reply. The sucking, glutinous mud is something for which the Somme offensive is remembered along with the enormous loss of life.

Cude was not alone in these experiences. Thousands of other messengers served on the Western Front. Arthur Roberts, born in Bristol in 1897, was working in Harland & Wolff Shipyard, Glasgow, when he volunteered to join the army in 1917. He enlisted with the 2nd Battalion Royal Scots Fusiliers and was sent to Belgium where he served in the fighting at Passchendaele. Arthur also kept a diary and in it he records that he had served as 'company-runner, batman, guide, dining-hall attendant, cycle-orderly, [anti-] aircraft-gunner, hut-builder, stretcher-bearer and one or two other things.' Soldiers were expected to be able to adapt to most types of tasks during the war and that included cycling.

Bicycle riders often found it easier to walk on foot rather than futilely struggle to pedal through a sea of mud. Indeed, some troops who were assigned to Cyclist Battalions from 1915 found they were such in name only and never received bicycles. Frank Dunham of the 25/London Regiment was sent to Belgium and had still not been issued with his bicycle a year later. He later recalled, 'there was never any issue of cycles to us.' Having been trained as infantry, that is exactly how his battalion served in the trenches in the area of Dickebusch about three miles south-west Ypres known as 'Dickebusch Huts' after the temporary accommodation erected there. Frank was promoted to sergeant and later placed in charge of the regimental aid post, a position which allowed him to use his first aid skills gained before the war to treat the wounded.

Chapter 4

Wheels and Wings

Pigeons had been used by the military for centuries to carry messages, but it was during the First World War that they really came into their own. Messengers would carry homing pigeons in small wicker paniers fitted to their bicycles. Messages could be attached to the legs of the birds and on being released they could fly hundreds of miles. Pigeons are highly intelligent, fast in flight, hardy and resilient.

The French army had developed the role of the pigeon as a means of delivering messages during the Franco-Prussian War of 1870–71, when they were used to fly messages out of Paris during the siege of 1871. All armies used them between 1914 and 1918. The British army had some

A pigeon is released to deliver a message. The bird could have been taken into the trench on a bicycle carrying the basket.

Cases such as this were used to carry pigeons in both world wars.

100,000 birds trained to fly to locations either in France or back to Britain. Special units were raised in all armies with trained handlers tending to the welfare of the birds.

The wicker panniers were designed to keep the birds secure, to prevent them being thrown around when travelling, and to keep the birds aired to prevent condensation which could affect their plumage and prevent flying. The bottoms of the baskets were made so that excretions could drop through to avoid the birds' plumage from becoming soiled. The baskets could be carried on a man's back or strapped to either the front or rear carrier of a bicycle. In 1915 the British army had fifteen 'pigeon lofts', each capable of holding 400 birds, mounted on vehicles for mobility, and an allocation of one handler to four birds. The handlers were issued with bicycles to carry small numbers of pigeons to a specific location where they would be released with their messages, or for purposes of liaising with other units using pigeons.

Italy joined the war on the side of the Allies in 1915, having prevaricated over which side with which to ally itself. It had close connections with Austria-Hungary and Allied commanders expected Italy to join the

Wicker baskets for carrying pigeons could be strapped to bicycles to transport the birds to trenches.

Central Powers. More than 5.6 million troops were mobilised of which over 460,000 were killed and 953,000 wounded during the fighting against the Austrian forces in the north of Italy and in the Alps. Under such conditions, use of bicycles was largely ruled out but some machines were used. The Italian army had become interested in creating cyclist units as a result of trials conducted by Lieutenant Luigi Camillo Natali in 1895. These came to the attention of General Eduardo Testafochi who arranged to expand the trials. They proved a success and led to the Italian army forming its first temporary cyclist unit, the 12th Regiment, at the musketry school based in Parma. In 1908 a man from this unit cycled 716 miles riding a machine produced by the company of Carraio which weighed sixty-six pounds. In 1910 the first Bersaglieri cyclist battalions were formed, each with three companies of 150 men.

The cyclist battalions had to be equipped with a suitable machine and in 1911 a competition was arranged to trial bicycles from eleven of the country's leading manufacturers. The trial was conducted over a course of 1,800 miles, following a route of unmade roads. The Bianchi Modello Militaire Brevettato (Model 1912) emerged the winner and the company was awarded a contract for 7,000 machines. Changes were made to provide improved springs and the government ordered a further 45,000 bicycles from Bianchi, as well as 1,500 motorcycles and 1,000 motor vehicles per year.

The bicycles were mostly issued to the 210,000 men serving with the 13 regiments of Bersaglieri which included 12 cycle battalions. In 1916 and 1917 the Bersaglieri would increase in strength to 15 and 16 regiments, while retaining 12 battalions of cyclist troops. In 1918 the Bersaglieri returned to 15 regiments and the cyclists were reduced to 8 battalions. The cyclist battalions mostly operated independently of their regiments. Serving in the 33rd Battalion of the 11th Regiment of Bersaglieri, which had an autonomous cyclist battalion, was Benito Mussolini, destined to later become El Duce, but it is unlikely he was ever required to ride a bicycle.

The Bersaglieri units suffered very heavy losses: 32,000 killed and 50,000 wounded, some of whom served in the Middle East during the Palestine Campaign of 1917 alongside British forces. The conditions in this theatre, being dry with hard compacted roads, were better suited for cyclists. The Italian army also used pigeons to send messages and cyclists would have carried birds with them in carrying baskets. It is understood that as many as 50,000 pigeons were used by the Italian army.

The German army used some 150,000 homing pigeons. In 1916 when the Portuguese army entered the war they used pigeons and had companies of cyclist troops. When America entered the war in 1917, the US Army used 20,000 pigeons.

The Japanese army secured a victory over Russia during the Russo-Japanese War of 1904–5 which saw both sides using bicycles in various roles. The victory led to Japan being established as a military power and coincided with a rapid expansion of its industry, which included the manufacture of bicycles.

Bicycles were used in the Balkan War of 1912, which saw Turkey, with allied support from Austria-Hungary, fighting against the 'Balkan League' of Bulgaria, Montenegro, Greece and Serbia. The cause of the war was age-old ethnic differences and regional disputes. It ended inconclusively, leading to another outbreak of fighting in 1913. Several of the countries

The Italian Bersaglieri Regiment moving forward with their bicycles. These men fought in northern Italy where the terrain was steep.

involved in these disputes would become involved in the World War, during which they continued to use bicycles.

The German government subsidised the manufacture of bicycles from the 1890s with the specific intention of using them for the military. Although German bicycle manufacturers rivalled those of France and Britain, when it came to creating specialist bicycles units the German army was a latecomer. This was about to change, with the publication of a treatise in 1898 entitled 'The Bicycle in the Service of the Armed Forces' in which the (anonymous) author suggests, 'the bicycle will have the same influence on the conduct of war as the railways have now,' and reminds his readers that originally the railways were not viewed as having a military application: 'the bicycle will have an effect on the future operation of war which will be as different to the present official military use of bicycles as the military use of railways in the 1840s was compared to today.'

The German military had begun serious experimenting with bicycles as a means of transportation in 1895 when the first official document 'Cycle Orders' appeared in May of that year. It identified the parts of the machine, handling abilities, training in their use and what equipment could be carried. Officers took part in exercises of speed and endurance, covering routes of difficult terrain over various distances.

German observers visiting South Africa during the Second Boer War saw bicycles in use with both the Boers and the British army. Other influences came from France in 1898, where news was released that the French army was creating companies equipped with bicycles for transportation. A report compiled for the German army carried a warning that if the French army used bicycles 'properly in a future campaign, France will be in a position to do Germany great damage'. The same document continues that the use of bicycles is 'a new form of warfare [which] will only be checked by establishing our own cycle troops as opposed to troops on cycles. It is difficult to tell how many these will be in total – 5,000 or more, as the French intend.' It sums up by stating Germany cannot have less than France and that training and preparation is essential.

Defeat in 1871 made France wary of its German neighbour, which continued to build up its armed forces. France implemented a series of changes and new weapons were introduced. One of the changes involved the creation of bicycle units. Since 1887 the French army had been conducting exercises using heavy-framed machines called the 'Bicyclette' produced by Peugeot, which by 1890 had been modified to become the 'Bicyclette Militaire'. Five years later, the standard model bicycle for the army was the 'Capitaine Gérard', named after Capitaine Henri Gérard of the 147 Infantry Regiment who had designed the machine. Between 1900 and 1920 the companies of Peugeot and Michelin would produce 46,000 Capitaine Gérards for the French army. It was with this machine that the French army went to war in 1914 and later supplied to the Russian and Romanian armies. Other types would also be used during the war, such as those produced by the French company of Gladiator, as were some types supplied by British factories.

Capitaine Henri Gérard was born in 1859, and attended the military academy of St Maixent in 1884. He was described as being 'a coach of men, [with] a fiery, kind and firm temperament'. He was well regarded by his fellow officers and the men who served under his command. As his military career advanced, so he developed a keen sense that bicycles had a military application, and at one point he commanded a unit of cyclist troops. In 1894 he wrote a treatise in which he examined 'the problem of the mounted infantry solved by the use of the bicycle'. Gérard's work led on to officers, such as General Hippolyte Langlois, the military scientist, formulating the 'Tactical consequences of the creation of the cyclist infantry'.

Gérard is also credited with developing a style of folding bicycle which was named after him (although he did not invent the folding design; that had been developed many years previously). He died in June 1908, before he saw the full effects of his creation coming together.

The first regular French cycling companies were raised and issued with bicycles in 1913. They were attached to Chasseurs battalions, which could be troops either horse-mounted or infantry. They soon acquired the nickname of 'wheeled hunters' – chasseur means hunter. French Divisional Headquarters had a Chasseur Cyclist Group attached which were *chasseur à pied* or infantry cyclists. A cyclist engineer group was also included in the divisional supply train.

From the very beginning of the war French army cyclists were being used as scouts to locate German positions and to carry messages. These units were attached to cavalry divisions serving in groups of up to 500 men. They could act as dismounted infantry to provide fire support in an attack and to give covering fire in rearguard actions when withdrawing. During the withdrawal to the Marne in the early months of the war cyclist infantry units held back the German advance to allow the main force to escape. One of these units was the 6th Cyclist Group which made one of the earliest contacts of the war with the German army and was able to report back to headquarters. These French units suffered a very high casualty rate.

One army which resisted the use of bicycles in the war was the American, even though pre-war trials had showed them to have a potential military role.

It was British military doctrine which shaped the structure of the armies of those countries in the British Empire and influenced the roles of troops and the type of weaponry and equipment they used. In Canada, five Cyclist Battalions were raised, along with a Canadian Reserve Cyclist Company. In India, where British troops used bicycles for a variety of duties, the use of the machines extended to the Calcutta Police. The Calcutta Volunteer Cyclists' Companies were issued with military versions of Raleigh bicycles shipped out from Britain between 1908 and 1910. Indian postal workers also used bicycles for delivering packages and letters.

In the first days of the war armies mobilised with troops using bicycles.

The first troops of the British Indian Army arrived in Belgium in September 1914 and by October some units, such as the 129th Baluchi (Duke of Connaught) Regiment had taken up positions in the front line in the area of Hollebeke, just south of Ypres. Some of the almost 29,000 troops in this first contingent were equipped with bicycles produced by BSA and they acquitted themselves admirably during the fighting of the winter of that year. The prewar levels of the British Indian Army had been around 155,000, but by 1918 more than one million Indian troops served overseas. The exact numbers that were mounted on bicycles or issued with the machines for use in the many theatres of war in which they fought has never been properly calculated and the true number remains unknown.

As the fighting spread to South Africa and the Middle East, between 1914 and 1918 the British army transported some 12,000 bicycles for use by troops in these theatres. In the Middle East, the Turkish army of the Ottoman Empire, and Germany's ally, were engaged by the British army in Mesopotamia (the area covered by modern day Syria, Jordan, Iran and Iraq).

The harsh conditions of the Gallipoli peninsula in April 1915 and the static trench warfare meant there was little or no use for bicycles, but that did not stop around 1,400 machines being sent there during the more than ten-month-long campaign.

Many of the troops who had fought at Gallipoli were ANZACs – the Australian and New Zealand Army Corps, formed from the Australian Imperial Force, AIF, and the New Zealand Expeditionary Force, NZEF. After Gallipoli the ANZACs found themselves back in Egypt, where they were reformed with replacements for those men lost in the fighting, re-equipped and given training in readiness to be sent to Europe. Among the new units to be raised in the reforming of the ANZACs were battalions of cyclist troops. In the case of the AIF, it expanded in size to five infantry divisions, each of which would include a company of cyclist troops, in keeping with the British New Army establishment adopted at the time which stipulated that each of these companies have six platoons with bicycles. Volunteers for these new companies were called for and the first units were raised between March and April 1916. Appointed commander of this new unit was Captain Jacob (Jack) Hindhaugh, who had enlisted in the Australian Light Horse and served in Gallipoli from where he was evacuated in July 1915 having been wounded. After his discharge from hospital Captain Hindhaugh was summoned to receive his orders, which he records in his diary for 14 March 1916: 'Went over to the 4th Light Horse, saw Stan, he said that the command of the Cyclist Corp is to be offered to me and I was to see Col. Foott in Cairo. Went in and had a talk to him. Have accepted it and I will leave with the 1st Division for France.' Each of the five companies had around 230 cyclists, which meant that, with officers, the combined strength was about 1,600 men. By mid-April 1916, Captain Hindhaugh with his 1st Division Cyclist Company had arrived in France. They were deployed to the south of Armentières where they were employed in diverse roles including reconnaissance, liaison and carrying messages.

In 1917 the Australian cyclist units were again reorganised and became the I ANZAC Cyclist Battalion commanded by Hindhaugh, by now promoted to major. He would end the war a lieutenant colonel. Following the assistance rendered by cyclist troops against the Germans, Major General W.P. Braithwaite wrote his gratitude on 31 July 1918: 'I have the honour to bring to the notice of the Corps Commander the services of the Cyclist Battalion, Corps Troops XXII Army Corps, under command of Major C.H. Evans DSO, which have been attached to the Division under my command during recent operations. Nothing could have been better than the fighting qualities displayed by, or the valour and endurance of, all ranks not only during the action of 23rd July, but throughout the subsequent fighting. I desire also to bring to the notice of the Corps Commander, the services of the Corps Mounted Troops, under Lieutenant Colonel Hindhaugh, who did valuable service throughout the time they were attached to the Division under my command. The men shewed enterprise and bravery while working in country difficult for cavalry. The patrols were boldly handled and sent back useful and accurate information.' The unit was disbanded in April 1919. More than 420,000 men served in the AIF. The cost was very high with 60,000 men killed and 137,000 wounded.

In April 1916 Major Charles Hellier Davis Evans of the NZEF was one of the officers to arrive in France at the head of one of the Divisional Cyclist Companies. When the New Zealanders had arrived in Egypt after their withdrawal from Gallipoli, like the Australians, they had formed the Divisional Cyclist Companies, equipped with 201 bicycles and six vehicles for the eight officers and 196 other ranks. Evans was informed that the units were to undergo changes in their structure. The changes, which also affected the Australian Cyclist Companies, saw the 1st Cyclist Battalion attached to the I ANZAC Corps while the 2nd Cyclist Battalion, with two companies of New Zealand troops commanded by New Zealand officers, was attached to the II ANZAC Corps. Each of the battalions comprised a headquarters and three companies, each of which was subdivided into three platoons, to give a complement of 26 officers and 310 other ranks. In addition, a new Cyclist Training Company was established in England for the purpose of preparing replacement troops before being sent to their battalions in Europe.

When the Australian Corps was formed in 1917 the 1st Cyclist Battalion was attached to it and when the II ANZAC Corps became the XXII Corps in 1918 the troops serving in the 2nd Cyclist Battalion were posted to other units of the AIF. Those New Zealand troops remaining were used to form the XXII Corps Cycle Battalion which would be commanded by the newly promoted Lieutenant Colonel Charles H.D. Evans. The men in this battalion were volunteers from the Mounted Rifles who, like their counterpart Australian Cyclist Companies, were being used as dismounted infantry, while those who retained their bicycles were used as dispatch riders when and where conditions allowed, along with other duties including reconnaissance. Being infantry, these troops were equipped with standard infantry weapons including the Lee-Enfield rifle, hand grenades and Lewis light machine guns.

In April and May 1918 the Germans mounted a series of attacks known collectively as the 'Ludendorff Offensive'. Lieutenant Colonel Evans's battalion, being part of XXII Corps, was involved in the fighting by supporting elements of the French 5th Army around Marfaux where they sustained heavy losses. A personal letter was sent to Evans by Brigadier General J.S. Bennett commanding 185 Brigade thanking him: 'Dear Evans, Now that you have left my Brigade I should like to thank both you and your men for the splendid work you did at Marfaux. You had a nasty job to do and you could not have done it better. Would you please let your officers and men know how much we appreciated all the help you gave us at a very trying time.'

During the war the ANZAC Cyclists Battalions earned many other letters praising them for their support, such as that sent by Lieutenant Colonel K.W. Moreland of X Corps in which he singles out the individual battalions of cyclists: 'It is difficult for me adequately to express to you my gratitude for the splendid work of the 1st, 2nd, 3rd and 4th Battalion, 3rd New Zealand (Rifle) Brigade and the II ANZAC Corps Cyclists… the keenness that they displayed is universally admired, and their skill is acknowledged to an example to any troops. Will you please tell these gallant men how much, while I deplore the casualties they suffered, I appreciate both their valuable work and their soldierly spirit.'

The ANZAC cyclist units were to remain engaged until the final stages of the war, by which time the 1st and 2nd Cyclist Battalions had lost 13 and 59 men killed. This may sound like low figures, but it should be remembered that these cyclist battalions were not as large as the standard infantry battalions, having a manpower level of perhaps fewer than 400 all ranks. The Australian Corps Cyclist Battalion was disbanded on 30 April 1919, having been in existence for just over one year, during which time some 3,000 men had served in the Australian Cycling Corps. New Zealand mobilised a total of 100,000 men during the war, of which 16,697 killed and 41,317 wounded, representing a casualty rate of 58 per cent.

Germany had overseas territories in the form of islands across the Pacific Ocean and four areas in Africa: Togoland (today known as Togo), Cameroon, and the larger states of German South-West Africa and German East Africa. Britain, France, Belgium and Portugal had possessions in Africa and the Pacific, and as the war widened into other theatres and fronts, so the Allies were forced to dispatch troops to protect these areas. After 1916 the Allies had to deploy ever-increasing numbers of troops to these areas, especially to Africa, along with weapons and equipment. However, the bicycle was not always useful in these theatres, as at Gallipoli, where there was very limited use for them.

On the outbreak of war, New Zealand, Australia and Japan sent warships to seize the German-owned Solomon Islands, Marianas and Samoa, which denied them being used as resupply and refuelling bases for German warships operating in the Pacific. In Africa, the German possessions of Togoland, Cameroon and German South-West Africa had coastlines facing west which would allow German warships to use these as supply bases from where they could threaten Allied shipping in the South Atlantic. On the east coast, German East Africa, with its port facilities at Dar es Salaam, Gazi, Mombasa and Tanga, could be used to supply warships operating against Allied shipping in the Indian Ocean.

The fighting in Africa was very different from the war in Europe where static trenches ran as demarcation lines between the Allies and the Germans. The African war was a war of movement, albeit at a very slow marching pace forced on the troops due to the heat and the harsh terrain. Horses and manpower provided by local tribespeople were mainly used for transportation of supplies. There was little opportunity for the use of bicycles here although there were some.

Operations in German South-West Africa were concluded by April 1915. Loss of access to this territory meant Germany was now deprived of the resources from the region, especially rubber for the tyres of vehicles and bicycles, and sisal fibre used in the manufacture of sacks and ropes. The German military commander in Africa was Paul von Lettow-Vorbeck. He had served in Africa before taking up his appointment to command the *Schutztruppe* in January 1914 and so knew something of the country and its terrain and conditions. When war broke out several months later, he was in a good position to begin operations against Allied interests in Africa. The Governor of German East Africa, Heinrich Schnee, advised adopting a defensive posture, but von Lettow-Vorbeck had other ideas and would conduct a guerilla-style campaign against the Allies. He would live off the land and use what supplies he captured from attacking Allied bases. At the beginning of 1916, after eighteen months of hard campaigning, Schnee had to concur with Vorbeck's tactics: '[we] get all we require from the country. We find all our food supplies and materials in our German East Africa.' He said that they found 'an unexpected wealth in this country such as we had never imagined in the past, and we find we have an adequate supply, even of such things as previously we thought it necessary to import'. By the end of the year things had changed: with resources running low and few supplies getting through, improvisations had to be made as logistical supplies were intercepted by the Allied naval blockade. The few bicycles that there were lacked tyres which needed sulphur for the vulcanising process.

Lettow-Vorbeck led his forces in a protracted campaign which tied down hundreds of thousands of Allied troops, keeping them away from the Western Front. Always on the move, the German commander destroyed railway lines, bridges and communications, never lingering to be engaged by superior forces. The British dispatched supplies to support their forces in South Africa, which included some 12,000 bicycles manufactured by the New Hudson Cycle Company at its factory in Birmingham.

In March 1916, Germany declared war on Portugal after mounting incursions into the Portuguese territory of Mozambique in east Africa. Portugal mobilised an Expeditionary Corps of 60,000. It included cyclist battalions. Most were sent to the Western Front but some were deployed to east Africa. Portuguese troops had been deployed to Mozambique and Portuguese Angola since 1914, with some 3,000 being transported by British ships.

Chapter 5

The Great War Continues

When Britain declared war on Germany on 4 August 1914, Canada was right there beside it, with Prime Minister William Lyon MacKenzie declaring war too. Canada had supported Britain during the Second Boer War, and in 1910 the Prime Minister at that time, Sir Wilfred Laurier, declared, 'When Britain is at war, Canada is at war. There is no distinction.' Canada became a Dominion in 1867 and many British citizens had emigrated there over the years, which forged these strong links. The country had a peacetime army of just over 3,100, with a voluntary militia force of 74,000, who were for home service.

The first troops were formed into the 1st Division of the Canadian Expeditionary Force with five officers and 88 other ranks being sent to Valcartier, Quebec, where they underwent basic training which lasted until September. On 29 September 1914 the first draft of 30,000 troops, among them the 1st Division Cyclist Company, began to embark on a fleet of thirty ships, arriving at Plymouth in England on 15 October. On disembarking they were sent to various camps such as Pond Farm and West Down South Camp on Salisbury Plain in Wiltshire, where they underwent further training and were issued with weapons and equipment.

A total of four Divisional cyclist companies would go on to be raised which had an initial combined strength of 31 officers and 738 other ranks, including NCOs, which would later increase to 1,200 men. A fifth unit, known as the Canadian Reserve Cyclist Company was raised at Shorncliffe, Kent, in April 1915, being formed using men drawn from the 9th, 11th, 12th and 17th Canadian Reserve Battalions. The following month the unit was sent to the British army's Cyclist Training Centre at Hounslow, where troops joining the Canadian Cyclist Companies would be trained in specific duties. From here, the unit was transferred to Larkhill in Wiltshire in November 1915, after which it was relocated to Chiseldon Camp in Swindon in February 1916. The final move came in

Repairing weapons and bicycles was an ongoing duty throughout the war.

October 1917 when it was sent to Seaford in West Sussex before being disbanded in February 1919.

The 1st Divisional Cyclist Company, commanded by Captain R.S. Robinson, was joined by the 2nd Divisional Cyclist Company commanded by Lieutenant Colonel G.Y. Denison in England in June 1915 with a compliment of 9 officers and 176 other ranks. The 3rd Divisional Cyclist Company arrived in England in January 1916 with 8 officers and 193 other ranks. After reorganization, which included receiving a new commanding officer, Captain L.P. Picard, at Swindon in February 1916, it was sent to France in March, being attached to the Canadian 3rd Division. The last Divisional Cyclist Company, the 4th, with 8 officers and 191 other ranks, arrived in England in May 1916. The unit was also sent to Chiseldon Camp where it was temporarily under the command of Captain G.B. Schwartz. The decision was taken to break up this company at Bramshott in Hampshire instead of attaching it to a Division and the troops absorbed into other units. This move may have been instigated because the Divisional Companies were to be organised into the newly created Canadian Corps Cyclist Battalion which was being formed.

Due to a combination of the small scale of the Divisional Cyclist Companies and the specialised support roles they were undertaking the units were suffering a disproportionate number of casualties. Sometimes they were spending several weeks under fire. The decision was taken to combine all Canadian cyclist companies into a single cyclist battalion. The men in the cyclist companies had undergone extensive training in Canada under the instruction of the Corps of Guides, which was part of the militia. Lessons included weapon handling, map reading, signalling and compiling reports, and first aid.

In May 1916 the Divisional Cyclist Companies were officially formed into the Canadian Corps Cyclist Battalion under the command of Major A. McMillan, at Abeele on the Franco-Belgian border. It became part of Brigadier General Raymond Brutinel's so-called 'Independent Force', also known as 'Brutinel's Brigade' or the 'Canadian Automobile Machine Gun Brigade'. The men saw service in the Ypres salient, Vimy Ridge and Passchendaele in 1917, where they suffered twenty-three per cent casualties, earning for themselves the nickname of 'The Suicide Squad'. One Canadian cyclist who served at Vimy Ridge remarked that most of the heights forming the feature ended up in sandbags which were used to construct their defensive positions. The cyclists in the Newfoundland Regiment suffered even higher casualties, in the order of ninety per cent. By 1918 the Canadian Expeditionary Force had mobilised 630,000 men, of which 424,000 served overseas; they suffered 67,000 killed and 173,000 wounded.

In November 1918, it is understood that a Canadian soldier by the name of Garnet W. Durham may have been the first Allied soldier to enter Germany after the signing of the Armistice when he rode a bicycle across the Bonn Bridge. The unit returned to Canada where it was demobilised in April 1919. The end finally came for the cyclist battalion on 15 November 1920 when under General Order 208 the unit was disbanded.

All armies of the belligerent nations used bicycle troops during the First World War, but the exact number of cyclists there were remains uncertain. It is believed that the figure for the British army may have been around 150,000. Around the same number of bicycles were used by the French and Belgians.

At the time of the outbreak of the war the bicycle was well proven as a useful form of transportation. Some of the designs were comparatively lightweight and journalists observing the early days of the war noted how Belgian troops carried their bicycles of the folding type, strapped to their backs. Some were as light as 30 pounds, and could be carried over obstacles such as walls or ditches before being remounted.

One of the major changes affecting cyclist troops in the British army came on 7 November 1914, three months into the war. This was Army Order 477, which authorised the formation of the Army Cyclist Corps. Here, for the first time, official orders were being issued for the creation of a regular army cyclist unit other than those formed among the Territorial units. This was followed by Army Order 478, which contained further details about the role of the unit and instructions on the duties it would undertake. Further details such as formation, equipment and pay were contained in this order. At the time of this order being issued, much of Belgium was under German occupation and the British army was determined to defend what was left of their ally's country.

What the Army Orders 477 and 478 meant was that those men serving with divisional cyclist companies were to be trained as cyclist infantry to serve with the companies as they were transferred to the Army Cyclist Corps. In 1914 there were approximately 13,000 cyclist troops in the British army, mainly serving with the Territorial Force. By 1915 this figure had risen to 30,000 with additional cyclist troops from Canada, New Zealand and Australia. New recruits volunteering could be enlisted into the Army Cyclist Corps with experienced officers being transferred from other regiments. Those men already serving with the fifteen Territorial cyclist battalions were unaffected by these Orders, but to a man they volunteered to serve overseas in the new formation. Basic pay was the same as in the infantry, one shilling a day, but once a man had qualified as a proficient cyclist he would qualify for special Proficiency pay.

The Army Cyclist Corps was issued with its own official cap badge for identification, the same as any other regiment. The centre of the design was a bicycle wheel with sixteen spokes overlaying two crossed rifles, above a scroll bearing the title of the regiment 'ARMY CYCLIST CORPS'. The wheel was surmounted by a king's crown. There were several versions issued, varying in style from a solid form to a pierced design. The design

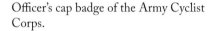

Officer's cap badge of the Army Cyclist
Corps.

Cap badge of other ranks in the Army
Cyclist Corps.

was worn by all ranks, but officers' versions often had a better finish. This replaced the cap badges worn by the Territorial battalions, such as the 8th (Cyclist) Battalion Northumberland Fusiliers, which later became the Northern Cyclist Battalion.

Hounslow Heath, on the outskirts of London, had been the site of a barracks and training camp for the British army since the eighteenth century for both infantry and cavalry. It was here in the First World War that the Army Cyclist Corps trained its recruits. Their training included trench fighting and treating wounded all in preparation to being sent to France or Belgium, or to the Middle East or later to Italy.

When the Territorial Force was established in 1908 it led to the formation of branches including the 7th (Cyclist) Battalion of the Devonshire Regiment, the Northern Cyclist Battalion and the Huntingdon Cyclist Battalion. The British army had had volunteer cyclist units among its numbers since the 1880s, and when war broke out in 1914 there were fifteen Territorial cyclist battalions. These were used for coastal defence work in the UK until 1915 when the Army Cyclist Corps was founded. In addition to this, one cyclist company had been formed in war time for each infantry division. So, for example, the structure of the 1st Division included the 1st Divisional Cyclist Company. These units were part of the regular army and all the new army divisions raised under Lord Kitchener's instructions in 1914 also included a cyclist company.

The men serving with the Territorial battalions were fully trained and equipped soldiers, but because of their status, being reserved for home defence, under the rules of the Territorial and Reserve Forces Act of 1907, that is the role to which they initially found themselves consigned. When they volunteered for overseas service each man received a small oblong-shaped silver metal badge bearing the words 'IMPERIAL SERVICE' over which was the King's crown. This was pinned on the right breast of the men's tunics to denote they were prepared for service wherever they would be sent. On the outbreak of war, the Territorial Force was divided into 1st Line service, which could see them being sent overseas, and 2nd Line service which meant they would only be deployed for home service. The 2nd Line category included those very few men, who for whatever reason, were not prepared to serve overseas, and others, who due to some form of physical restriction, or employed in essential war work, were kept back.

By the end of 1914 the British army had suffered very heavy losses and replacement troops were needed urgently. The trained soldiers of the Territorial Force who had volunteered for overseas service were sent to France and Belgium, which left behind the Home Service soldiers to mount coastguard duties to alert against possible German actions, including air raids and any naval bombardments of the coastline. Being mounted on bicycles, they were mobile and could report quickly. A 3rd Line was formed later from which trained men could be taken to replace losses in the first two Line services. When the Army Cyclist Corps was formed in 1915, trained soldiers from the Territorial Force were taken from their battalions to be used as instructors at Hounslow along with other training staff.

Secretary of State for War Lord Haldane created the Territorial Force in 1908. Initially, ten cyclist battalions were raised, one from the 26th Middlesex, five from volunteer battalions, and four newly formed, each of which had regimental affiliations. This figure would increase to fourteen cyclist battalions before the outbreak of war when the Northern, Highland, Kent, and Huntingdonshire Cyclists, which were independent battalions, were raised but had no regimental affiliations. In 1914, when Army Orders 477 and 478 were issued, they became part of the Army Cyclist Corps (ACC) and were given the cap badge of this new formation. As trained soldiers with knowledge in tactics using bicycle drills, some of these men formed the central core of instructors to train the new formation. Sportsmen who had been racing cyclists before the war joined the Army Cyclist Corps, training new recruits to improve their stamina. When the new battalions of the ACC were formed, each comprised companies of fifty men.

While cyclist troops had not been used in a direct combat role during the Second Boer War, they had provided vital service in other duties, including reconnaissance and communications. It was decided to use the cyclist battalions in those roles for which they had proved themselves best suited. The 10th (Cyclist) Battalion Royal Scots was one of the new units to be raised as part of the Haldane Reforms of 1908, with eight companies each of fifty men. It came under Scottish Command and had been preceded by a short-lived Cyclist Company which existed between 1900 and 1906. Three new battalions were created for the ACC, these being the 1st/10th, 2nd/10th and 3rd/10th.

The 1st and 2nd Battalions of the 10th remained in the vicinity of Berwick where they conducted patrols and other home defence duties. In early 1918 they were dispatched to Ireland. The 3rd/10th Battalion was disbanded in March 1916, with its members being transferred to either the remaining two battalions or the Machine Gun Corps. Another Scottish cyclist unit was the 8th (Cyclist) Battalion, Black Watch (Royal Highlanders), which separated from its regimental affiliation in 1909 and became known as the Highland Cyclist Battalion comprising the usual eight companies, coming under Scottish Command on the outbreak of war before becoming part of the ACC in 1915. The 1st/1st Highland Cyclist Battalion was retained on Home Defence duties until May 1918 when it was posted the Ireland. The 2nd/1st Battalion had a similar history, except that some of its troops were sent to form the 1st Provisional Cyclist Company in July 1915, but this was disbanded in April 1916. The 3rd/1st was a holding unit to provide troops for the other battalions. It was disbanded in March 1916, with its troops being sent to either the other two battalions or to the Machine Gun Corps.

The 5th (Cyclist) Battalion East Yorkshire Regiment was another of those Territorial Force units created in 1908 and had a history which could be traced back to 1859. However, it failed as a battalion of the ACC and in March 1915 only a single battalion, the 1st/5th, had been raised with eight companies and an HQ Company. Further battalions could not be formed due to low numbers of recruits caused by the men rushing to enlist in other regiments. The 1st/5th Battalion remained assigned to Home Defence duties for the duration. The 8th (Cyclist) Battalion had a regimental affiliation with the Northumberland Fusiliers, but it separated in 1910 to become the Northern Cyclist Battalion with the customary eight companies, formed in alphabetical order from A to H. They were posted across Northumberland to areas such as Blyth, where they conducted home defence duties. Like the other ACC battalions, it had three battalions, known as the 1st/1st Northern Cyclist Battalion, 2nd/1st and 3rd/1st. When war was declared the whole battalion was posted to Morpeth. In 1915 it became part of the ACC and the following year the 1st/1st was posted to Alnwick where it undertook home defence duties. In 1915 some troops from the 2nd/1st were sent to Chapel St Leonards where they joined the 10th Provisional Cyclist Company, with the remainder being posted to Sheerness in 1916 where they remained on home defence duties for the duration. The 3rd/1st was raised in July 1915 and used as a holding battalion to provide troops for the other two battalions. It was disbanded in March 1916 and, like the 10th (Cyclist) Battalion Royal Scots, the troops were either sent to the 1st and 2nd battalions or the Machine Gun Corps.

The other Cyclist Battalions were organised along similar lines and the troops deployed to various roles and duties accordingly. This included the 6th (Cyclist) Battalion, Norfolk Regiment, 7th (Cyclist) Battalion, Devonshire Regiment, 9th (Cyclist) Battalion, Hampshire Regiment, 7th (Cyclist) Battalion, Welsh Regiment, and the 8th (Cyclist) Battalion, Essex Regiment. Two battalions of the 25th (County of London) Kent Cyclist Battalion, London Regiment would later serve in the Third Anglo-Afghan War of 1919. Some troops serving with these Cyclist Battalions did see action, where they served as dismounted infantry due to the conditions of trench warfare. Between May and June 1916, divisional cyclist companies were formed to become cyclist battalions for each corps headquarters as part of the Army Cyclist Corps which were used to reinforce divisional cavalry squadrons, serving with the military police, to direct traffic and units to their positions, and provide working parties to assist divisional engineers. Cyclist troops could be allocated to other roles, but their fundamental roles remained as messengers, scouting and security patrols, especially along canal systems which were used as transportation arteries to move supplies and as such were vulnerable to enemy sabotage.

The Huntingdonshire Cyclist Battalion was raised in February 1914 and comprised three battalions, numbered 1/1st, 2/1st and 3/1st. It was this unit which had the distinction of being the first to have the nickname 'Gaspipe Cavalry' applied to it. Although the 1/1st Battalion was mobilised on 4 August 1914, the very day war was declared, it did not leave England but served at various locations in the North-East. In 1916 it provided around 600 men to serve with the 1/8th Battalion Royal Warwickshire Regiment for service on the Western Front in France. The 2/1st Huntingdonshire Cyclist Battalion was raised in October 1914 and, being rated as a 2nd Line battalion, like its sister battalion the 1/1st, it spent the duration of the war on home defence duties which included cycle patrols along the north-east coast. The third battalion, the 3/1st, was raised in 1915 and was used to provide replacement troops to the other two battalions. It was disbanded in March 1916 with the remaining men being sent either to the 1/1st and 2/1st Battalions, or as replacement to battalions of the Machine Gun Corps on the Western Front.

Across Britain, recruiting posters were stuck on walls and advertisements appeared in specialist cycling magazines and other publications of the day. In these, announcements were made extolling 'Cyclists! Use your skill for your Country' by enlisting in the Army Cyclist Corps. One poster announced: 'A Few Smart Men Wanted for The London Cyclists'. This call was for men to enlist in the 25th City of London Cyclist Battalion the London Regiment. These advertisements were enthusiastically answered with men coming forward to join the army and being posted to cyclist units. A poster appealing for men to enlist with the South Midland Divisional Cyclist Company asked two questions of potential recruits: 'Are you fond of cycling?' and 'If so, why not cycle for the King?' It ended with: 'Bad teeth no bar.' At the time the physical health of potential recruits was often very poor, with men being underweight and dental hygiene ranging from inadequate to non-existent. Enlisting in the army would provide remedial dental care. Being underweight was not deemed to be too debilitating; in any case, a better diet would soon take care of most problems.

In an official communication dated 20 November 1914, the commander of the British army, Field Marshal Sir John French, noted: 'I am anxious in this despatch to bring to your Lordship's special notice the splendid work which has been done throughout the campaign by the Cyclists of the Signal Corps. Carrying despatches and messages at all hours of the day and night in every kind of weather, and often traversing bad roads blocked with transport, they have been conspicuously successful in maintaining an extraordinary degree of efficiency in the service of communications. Many casualties have occurred in their ranks, but no amount of difficulty or danger has ever checked the energy and ardour which has distinguished this corps.'

A recruiting poster of the British army appealing for recruits to enlist as cyclists.

Recreated Army Cyclist Corps of the First World War with typical bicycle of period complete with brackets for carrying weapons.

Recreated scene showing how the Army Cyclist Corps would have pedalled to war.

A recreated Army Cyclist Corps member on his bicycle which is carrying his rifle and other kit.

This acknowledgement of the value of cyclists was shared among officers. Not all committed their recognition to paper in written communication, but such high opinions would continue to be held throughout the duration of the war.

In 1920 the ACC was disbanded, the battalions being merged with regular units such as the 25th (County of London) Cyclist Battalion which joined the Royal Corps of Signals. In 1922, all the Territorial cyclist battalions still remaining were converted back to conventional units. The Cyclist Battalions would not be reformed in the future, a move followed by other countries such as Canada and New Zealand which had similar formations. Bicycles would continue to be used in future conflicts, but on a much reduced scale.

The legacy left by the men who served in the ACC and other similar units is indelible, the evidence of which appears today on the headstones in many of the Commonwealth War Graves Commission cemeteries across France and Belgium. Private W. Liddell 3149 of the ACC serving with the 9th Division in Madagascar Trench, near Auchy-les-Mines, during the Battle of Loos in September 1915 was awarded the Distinguished Conduct Medal 'for conspicuous gallantry'. His citation appeared in the *London Gazette* on 11 March 1916: 'hearing a wounded man from another battalion who was lying out in the open, calling for assistance, he [Liddell], accompanied by Captain Campbell, jumped over the parapet, and together they carried the man to safety.' By the time the citation appeared, Liddell was dead, having been killed on 25 February 1916. His headstone can be found at Gunners Farm Cemetery in Belgium. There are hundreds more headstones bearing the cap badge of the Army Cyclist Corps.

Some have no known grave, such as 19-year-old Private Ernest Leonard Gays serving with the Northern Cyclist Battalion, who was attached to X Corps when he was killed on 18 August 1917 during the Battle of Passchendaele. He was buried by his friend Private James Smith who was serving with him in the same unit. He recalled how he took his friend's body 'by the ankles, the other two took him by the arms, and we laid him in and covered him up. I remember feeling a bit upset, for the grave was only about four feet deep. I knew he probably wouldn't be there for very long, because of the shell-fire.' He was correct in his assumption, the grave being lost in the fighting. Today Private Smith's name, along with those of Corporal Bernard Palin, Privates W.H. French and A. Rostron, and Lieutenant A.F. Blyth, who also served with the Northern Cyclist Battalion, appear on the memorial panels at Tyne Cot CWGC cemetery in Belgium.

Private James (Jimmy) Smith had enlisted with the Northern Cyclist Battalion and together with Ernest Gays ended up serving as 'dismounted' infantry engaged in the fighting around Bellewaerde Wood in May 1915. Private W.G. Bell, serving with the 9th Battalion Army Cyclist Corps, remembered how up to 300 men from his battalion rode their bicycles towards the Front Line, where they dismounted, leaving them in a collection area, and marched forward to the trenches to fight as infantry. In the trenches they did the same work as other men by digging new trenches and repairing the old earthworks. After working through the day, the men would march back, collect their bicycles and return to the rear area. Private Smith remembered digging trenches at the fiercely fought over location known as 'Hill 60', just south of Ypres. Like most cyclist troops, he was to spend days engaged in this role. In this they were the same as any other trained riflemen – after all, they were infantry first and foremost – but with bicycles serving to get them to their destination.

In contrast to the British or French armies, the German army had bided its time before committing itself to the introduction of bicycles into the military. They had been sufficiently interested to conduct military exercises. One trial in 1894 involved Bavarian infantry using machines fitted with solid tyres, but they performed less well than expected. The following year another exercise was conducted, this time with bicycles fitted with pneumatic tyres. The result was a vast improvement in performance and it caused many observers who had previously had doubts to change their minds about the bicycle.

In 1898 the German army finally conceded and agreed to accept bicycles into service for a limited period during which they would conduct trials. These machines were commercially available civilian models known as 'Roadsters', rugged, heavy duty designs lacking refinements, which fitted them perfectly for the army. It also meant that any deficiency in military requirements could be made up by requisitioning civilian machines.

By 1914 there were thirty-six independent companies of cyclist infantry with each cavalry unit having a battalion of cyclists attached to serve as infantry and provide fire support. There were further reserve cyclist companies and trained infantry to provide replacements for losses.

The bicycle they used was known as the Herrenrad Victoria 'Model 12', weighing 14 kg. It could be equipped with carriers to transport baskets for carrier pigeons, and dispatch cases could be attached to the crossbar for messengers carrying orders. They had 28-inch wheels and a 24-inch frame. Later in the war the Allied blockade prevented rubber from Africa being imported which led to a shortage of tyres. Special wheels were devised with double rims which held a 'sandwich' of springs around the circumference to serve as a shock absorber. This emergency measure was time-consuming in factory assembly, and as a shock absorber it was never as good as pneumatic tyres with rubber inner tubes.

As the war progressed, the number of cyclist units increased. Their roles mirrored those of cyclists in other armies: mostly messengers, reconnaissance and liaison duties. They were trained and armed as infantrymen, and fought as such when dismounted. An increase in demand for bicycles was met by taking machines from civilians in the areas of France and Belgium under German occupation. This eased the pressure on German factories manufacturing bicycles, allowing them produce other essential material, such as weapons.

One messenger serving in the Bavarian Infantry Regiment 16 was Adolf Hitler, posted to Ypres in Belgium in 1914, where he served as a *Radfahrer bis Regiment* or regimental cyclist.

Small two-wheeled trailers which could be towed behind bicycles when conditions allowed were developed to transport light loads of medical supplies and rations. But it was soon realised that using trailers would never work and the idea was dropped. So too was the notion of machine guns mounted on two-wheeled carriages being towed behind bicycles. The only multi-wheeled versions of the bicycle used during the First World War were the ambulance combinations used to evacuate the wounded.

All armies used bicycles fitted with reels mounted on brackets to allow telephone cables to be laid so that field telephones could be connected.

Chapter 6

Other Services Needed Bicycles

Outside the military, the usefulness of the bicycle became widely and quickly recognised by other branches of official services and organizations. The Boys Brigade, founded in 1883, and the Boy Scouts, founded in 1908, taught military-style skills to boys, including map reading, field-craft and first aid. Some of the members of these organizations were fortunate to have their own bicycles which allowed them to lend their services to the military during the war to deliver messages. They also supported the Territorial Volunteers, with more than 1,400 assisting with Home Service duties.

The Boy Scouts had grown quickly, gaining an international following with groups being established in France, Belgium, Germany, Japan and America. The girls had their equivalent known as 'Girl Guides'. All countries used the services of the Boy and Girl Scouts, encouraging them by appealing to their patriotism to support their countries by using their bicycles. They were able to ride their bicycles to deliver the hundreds of telegrams and messages which were daily being sent to hospitals and police stations. In Britain, those who were engaged in war work were given a special red badge to wear on their uniform. By 1918 over 80,000 such badges had been awarded. Messages of gratitude were received, such as: 'Please tell Baden-Powell that I don't know how we should get on without these little chaps.'

The emergency services in all countries used bicycles in addition to motorised transport, including the ambulance services. The police, from the first days of the war, increased their patrols around vulnerable locations such as gas works, port installations and bridges. To meet this need, the Metropolitan Police in London recruited 1,000 new constables. Police forces across the country faced a manpower shortage as over 4,000 constables left to enlist. Constables on patrol were able to extend the range of their 'beat' with bicycles. This increased mobility allowed them to

During the First World War millions of factory workers rode bicycles, such as these women working in a munitions factory.

patrol the docks to prevent sabotage and theft which would have affected the war effort. There was still a shortage of manpower. This was remedied by the increased use of women police officers.

Margaret Damer Wilson and Mary Sophia Allen, both from well-to-do families, established the 'Women's Police Volunteers' in 1914. They were joined in their efforts by Nina Boyle, who called for women to become 'special constables'. Around 4,000 women enlisted with the police force during the war. They became known as the Women's Police Service after the war. The presence of women police officers allowed the better control of female drunkenness and prostitution. Another function was to keep order among the growing number of women working in factories to produce ammunition, weapons and uniforms. To allow them to conduct these duties the women were often required to ride bicycles.

One completely new duty for the police was air raid warning. Since 1914 the Germans had been sending massive airships – Zeppelins – to bomb targets as widely dispersed as Great Yarmouth in Norfolk, Tynemouth and London. 'Blackouts' were introduced to prevent the airships from identifying targets: curtains had to be drawn and no light was allowed to be seen from outside. Constables would patrol streets on bicycles to see

Women like this munitions worker did long hours, including night shifts, and a bicycle would provide transport to get home.

that the regulations were being obeyed. Also they would shout warnings of air raids. On 16 December 1914, three German warships shelled Hartlepool, Scarborough and Whitby, killing 78 people and injuring 228. The police had to help in clearing up the devastation and remain vigilant in case of another attack. Bicycles kept them mobile.

Postal workers traditionally used bicycles to deliver the mail. Many postal workers left to join the armed forces during both world wars. In Britain in the first war 75,000 postal workers enlisted and some 8,500 would be killed. Postal workers had a long tradition of military service, either enlisting during time of war or gaining employment with the Post Office after completing military service. In either case, the men had knowledge of riding bicycles. On 4 August 1914, the day war was declared, postmen across Britain delivered over 100,000 telegrams to the reservist troops with instructions for them to report to their regimental depots.

Connections between the military and the Post Office went back to 1868, when the Post Office Rifles was raised as a volunteer regiment, being known at the time as the 49th Middlesex Rifles. When the Territorial Force was created the regiment became the 8th (City of London) Battalion or Post Office Rifles. With their skills and knowledge in handling bicycles the obvious choice for many was to join the Army Cyclist Corps. Post Office workers suffered casualties on the Home Front as well as on the battlefield, such as Postman Albert Beal who was killed during the shelling of Scarborough on 16 December 1914 while delivering letters.

As well as the police force, women also joined the post office. They now became a familiar sight riding bicycles to deliver letters.

The greatest user of bicycles in both world wars in every belligerent nation was the workforce. Traditionally, factory workers had either walked or used public transport, such as trams or omnibuses, to get to their place of employment. The bicycle gave them independent mobility and some workers in factories with a shift pattern alternating between night and day would share their machines. Their bicycles were often second-hand or rescued from the scrap heap and repaired. Hundreds of thousands of bicycles were owned by the workforce in every country, especially those more advanced such as Britain, France and Germany. They allowed women more choice when entering the work place. In Britain some

50,000 women were employed in the public transport sector by 1918. During the war, more than a million women entered factories to produce guns, ammunition and uniforms.

Companies which had been producing bicycles before the war diversified into the production of other essential war materiel, including shells for artillery, motor vehicles and engines for aircraft, while continuing to produce bicycles for the military. During the war it is estimated that Britain supplied some 100,000 bicycles to Belgium, France, Italy, Rumania, Russia and even America. Britain also supplied bicycles to the armies of other Allied countries, such as Serbia, Portugal and Greece.

King's Norton Metal Company of Birmingham, was established in 1889 by Thomas Richard Bayliss and Thomas Abraham Bayliss, a father and son partnership, to produce ammunition and weapons. The company also produced wire and tubes which were used in bicycles, employing several thousand new workers.

In the years after the war, the labour force in Britain and in most European countries was kept mobile due to the bicycle. Throughout the Second World War, which saw a gigantic surge in the levels of employment in factories, bicycles provided a cheap, simple means of transportation requiring no fuel. The bicycle on the Home Front during both world wars allowed the workforce to produce the supplies, weapons and ammunition it did, and in that sense it is rather unfairly overlooked in the part it played in the Allied victories.

Chapter 7

Evacuation of the Wounded

The faster a wounded man can be evacuated to a base hospital for treatment the greater are his chances of survival. One nineteenth century surgeon who knew this all too well was Baron Dominique Jean Larrey, who served with Napoleon's Grande Armée on many campaigns. He set about developing improved ambulance wagons which provided comfort during transportation. The best vehicles of Larrey's day were those with side-by-side wheels drawn by horses.

When the first bicycles appeared, with their linear wheel arrangement, the configuration did not lend them to the evacuation of the wounded. Over time it was discovered that if two machines could be attached together side by side using a framework, the improvisation would create a stable platform with four wheels. Such a use had already been speculated by Lieutenant Colonel Savile in his presentation on the military role of the bicycle in 1887 and later by Baden-Powell. An 'ambulance bicycle' was developed by the British company of Alldays in 1894, which mounted a stretcher on two wheels and was pushed like a handcart. This was followed in 1895 with a design which joined two bicycles together side by side, just as Savile had suggested.

One of the first institutions to use Alldays' design was the Birmingham Hospital Saturday Fund. The idea was quickly taken up and by 1898 its use was spreading. In the bustling American city of Chicago, Dr John T. Hinckley used a combination of two tandem bicycles to demonstrate the speed such a design could convey a stretcher. Two of the four riders were medically trained in the treatment of injured patients and showed how the machine could be ridden along a route three miles long in busy traffic in around sixteen minutes. In one month one machine was used to transport more than 100 patients to the hospital. It could also carry equipment to treat the patient during the trip, such as bandages and sutures.

Other emergency services saw the benefits offered by this combination and soon police forces were using 'bicycle ambulances' to support medical emergencies. Red Cross Societies used the combination and the military adopted it too.

Dr Hinkley's trials showed great promise but they were conducted under peacetime conditions far removed from the chaos and dangers of the battlefield, where the ground could be torn up by craters and trenches. During the First World War, one Frank Dunham served in a Cyclist Battalion of the British army. Coming from a middle-class family and being a deeply religious man he joined a Red Cross unit as a volunteer at the start of the war. Thinking that his medical training would be best used in the army he enlisted in the 25th (County of London) (Cyclists) Battalion of the London Regiment. However, as he soon discovered, not everyone who served in these units was issued with a bicycle. Given the conditions of the battlefields it was not easy for bicycles to be used for the evacuation of the wounded, nor for that matter, any of the other roles for which it had been identified.

Recovering the wounded from the battlefield could be time consuming and labour-intensive. Private F. Hodgson serving with the 11th Canadian Field Ambulance of the Canadian Army Medical Corps as a stretcher-bearer in Belgium during the Battle of Passchendaele in October 1917, later recalled how difficult it was for six men to carry one wounded man on a stretcher through the sea of mud. After hours of struggling they reached the Casualty Clearing Station, by which time their patient had died. Under such conditions, where men and animals floundered, motor vehicles certainly could not have coped. But bicycles were used to transport stretchers to the Front Line.

On good roads, bicycle ambulances would have been a useful supplement to motorised transport, but as a sole means of evacuating the wounded they would not have kept pace with the numbers involved. Even without the cloying mud they would have fallen short. As well as using recognised conversions, using four bicycles, some armies improvised bicycle ambulances using anything which was available. The French army, for example, would secure two bicycles together side by side using rope and either wooden or metal poles, from which they would suspend a canvas sheet, like a sailor's hammock, in which the patient could be carried. Rifles could be used instead of poles if nothing else was available and service greatcoats would serve in place of canvas. It was usually impossible to ride the combination when conditions were muddy, and cyclist medics had to cooperate in pushing. Even under firm dry conditions, it was difficult for multiple riders to pedal in unison and steer together.

The Hungarian army used a purpose-built design comprising a trailer-stretcher mounted on a pair of wheels and towed behind a bicycle. Some designs mounted stretchers on bicycle-style wheels attached to the handlebars and were pushed forward in front of the rider. The stretcher could be covered by a canvas screen to shelter the patient and a fourth castor-type wheel fitted to support the front end of the stretcher. These designs were still being used by some armies during the Second World War. The designs were always best suited to level roads: to pedal uphill with such a heavy load was physically demanding if not impossible, and when descending the load could be virtually uncontrollable.

Ambulance bicycles, while a good idea in principal, proved impractical under battle conditions. The number of wounded troops evacuated by them was small compared to that transported by motorised ambulances.

Artist's impression of a wounded soldier being evacuated by stretcher. He has included bicycles propped against the trees. Bicycles could be used to evacuate the wounded too.

As an alternative means of transport, when nothing else was available, they could be pressed into use, but only when road conditions were favourable. The fact that the idea continued for so long shows that the idea was viable, but in the end it was the motor vehicle which proved more efficient. During the Second World War, motorised ambulances reduced transportation time to treatment centres and improved the survival rate.

In the mid-1930s as the political situation deteriorated and the threat of another war increased, poison gas became a great fear. Millions of respirators were issued in many European countries, especially Britain where there was a national distribution. How to evacuate casualties affected by gas was a concern. One idea was a special stretcher encased in a canvas cover mounted on the front of a tricycle. The patient would be laid on the rigid stretcher base and sealed off by the canvas side screens to prevent contamination. The tricycle had two wheels at the front and one at the rear. The front end of the stretcher unit was supported by a single castor-type wheel. The rider could steer the machine using a bar fitted to the carrier. The idea was well-intentioned, but it is doubtful it would have

Recreated combination developed for use to evacuate victims of poison gas attack in the Second World War, but never used.

The gas victim evacuation stretcher and bicycle combination seemed a useful idea, but it was never put to the test.

It would have been difficult to imagine a fleet of these combinations evacuating victims for treatment if poison gas had been used.

proved functional in practice. Anyway, poison gas was never used in the war and the carrier never deployed in its intended role.

Daily life in the trenches of the Western Front often saw men reduced to living semi-subterranean existences plagued by lice and rats. Many men wished for a transfer, but very few managed to get a new posting. One man fortunate enough to obtain a transfer was Captain William Watson. In late 1916 he was commanding a company in a battalion of the Cyclist Corps attached to XI Corps when he heard about the tanks operating at the Battle of the Somme. It was the first time tanks had been used in action. From what he heard Captain Watson was sufficiently convinced that serving in tanks was a preferable way of fighting the war. He wrote: 'We learned... the approximate shape and weight of tanks. We pictured them and wondered what a cyclist battalion could do against them. Apparently the tanks had not been a great success on the Somme, but we imagined potentialities. They were coloured with romance that had long ago departed from the war. An application was made for volunteers.'

Soldiers carried medical kits to treat the wounded and German cyclist troops had their kits stored to hand ready to use on the crossbar.

The term *Verbandkasten* means first aid kit. It was carried in a handy container attached to the crossbar.

If the Germans used tanks, Watson did not relish the idea of having to tackle them from the saddle of a bicycle. He did obtain his transfer and survived the war. Later he wrote *A Company of Tanks*, a memoir of his time as a tank commander. The XI Corps, with which Captain Watson had been serving, was transferred to the Italian Front in December 1917, taking with it a battalion of the Cyclist Corps.

Chapter 8

America Fights and the End of the War

On the other side of the Atlantic, in America, few wanted to get involved in the war. Americans saw the war as a European affair and of no concern to them. However, after the sinking of the *Lusitania* and the discovery of the Zimmerman Telegram, President Woodrow Wilson had no option but to declare war on Germany on 6 April 1917.

In 1914 the US Army stood at around 98,000 men. Even when counting the 27,000 members of the National Guard, it was still smaller than the Belgian army.

Within four months of declaring war there were 14,000 troops of the American Expeditionary Force, as it was known, in France. By the end of 1917 this figure had risen to 182,000. By 1918 America had mobilised four million men, of which two million were serving in France.

Orders for military equipment were placed, ranging from boots and uniforms to vehicles, including bicycles. Several manufacturers were approached, including Westfield producing Columbia bicycles, Great Western, Harley-Davidson and the Davis Sewing Machine Company, receiving orders amounting to 67,500 machines. In 1906 the Davis Sewing Machine Company was producing bicycles at the rate of 600 machines per day, and an equal number of sewing machines.

By the end of the war however, in November 1918, only 29,504 bicycles of the contract had been delivered, of which just 3,252 were produced by the Davis Sewing Machine Company. The US Army did not establish bicycle units along the same lines as other Allied nations and by the end of the war only 26,407 machines had been sent to France, where they were used for delivering messages around camps and airfields and in other roles of minor importance. The US Army much preferred to use petrol driven motor vehicles, including motorbikes such as those produced by Harley-Davidson. These were used for delivering messages, liaison duties, carrying passengers in sidecar combinations, and even the evacuation of wounded soldiers. They could also deliver medical supplies and other essential items. The Indian Motorcycle Company supplied motorbikes to the army with sidecars which were adapted to mount machine guns.

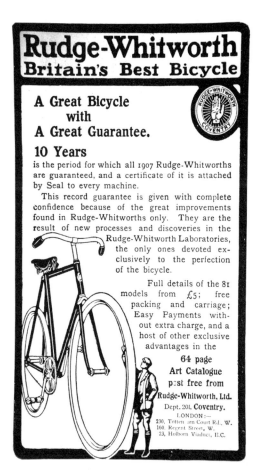

Adverts were intended to increase sales of bicycles and raise interest.

Manufacturers used adverts to make their bicycles sound the best.

Chapter 9

The Wheels Turn Again 1930–45

After the end of the Great War in 1918, all nations began to shed troops and reduce the size of their armies. In Britain, by 1920, the strength of the regular British army had been reduced to around 435,000 and two years later this figure was halved, making it smaller than it had been at the start of either the Crimean War or the Second Boer War. With former enemy states now disarmed most countries did not see the need for large armies. France was alone in maintaining a large standing army, with some 900,000 troops, and ordered the building of a series of defensive fortifications in depth known as the Maginot Line along the border with Germany.

In the Netherlands, which had been neutral during the Great War, the strength of the army stood at 8,000 professional officers, NCOs and enlisted men who trained the annual intake of 60,000 conscripts, who would add to the numbers of reservists to take the number up from 114,000 to 270,000 men who could be mobilised in a crisis. In 1939 the Dutch army had 150,000 bicycles, more than enough to provide for two years' conscript intake.

In Belgium, which had suffered so greatly between 1914 and 1918, the country reaffirmed its neutrality status and the level of the army was reduced to 100,000 troops, which was less than pre-war strength.

Sweden was also a neutral country, but because of its geographical location, being so far to the north isolated from western European states, it had never seen the need to undertake radical changes to its army. The only major change in modern times had been made in 1901 when the horses of cavalry support of the 27th Gotlandic Infantry Regiment were replaced by bicycle troops. In 1940 the country could call on 400,000 men increasing to 600,000 with full mobilisation. It had many types of armoured vehicles, including tanks, which had a bicycle squadron attached to its cavalry battalions. The cyclist units were used during the summer months, but in winter the units converted to mechanised.

In Sweden in 1942 there were six bicycle infantry regiments, *cykelskyttebataljon*, using either the m/30 machine weighing 52 pounds or the m/42 weighing 57 pounds. The Swedish army used several designs of bicycle, including machines produced in Italy by Bianchi. Other designs

This recreated image, using original equipment, shows how the Swedish army used troops on bicycles to patrol the border with Norway which was under German occupation.

This recreated image shows how the Swiss army used bicycles to patrol their national border.

were produced in Finland and a German design was built under licence with some modifications. The company of Husqvarna produced the m/42 for which it also developed a light-weight collapsible two-wheeled trailer which could be towed behind it and later models such as the m/104A and m/105A. The trailer was known as the S/78 and could be used to transport loads of ammunition and food or, in an emergency, a patient on a stretcher.

The Swiss army also had a small cargo trailer known as the Anhanger, which could be towed by the MO-5 bicycles (Militaer Ordinanz-05) and used for the same purposes.

Other companies producing bicycles for the Swedish army included Monark and Nymans, and together with Husqvarna these remained the most widely used service bicycles. The Swedish army also modified some machines into so-called tandem designs for radio operators to carry their equipment. Another design joined two bicycles together with connecting brackets to link the leading machine to the front of the bicycle following behind. This allowed a stretcher to be carried to evacuate a wounded man. Unfortunately the design was not self-supporting, unlike the side-by-side configuration as used by the French army which provided a stable platform. The Swedish method of transporting a stretcher using two bicycles was functional, but the French design for casualty evacuation was more practical. In the event, Sweden was never engaged in the fighting between 1939 and 1945, but it still had to maintain patrols along the border it shared with Norway which was occupied by the German army from 1940 until 1945. Undertaking these duties were cyclists of the Swedish army.

During the 1930s as Italy and Germany led by Benito Mussolini and Adolf Hitler built up their powerful modern armies, they included bicycles.

Japan, which, like Italy, had been an ally with Britain and France in the 1914–1918 war, was becoming increasingly militaristic and belligerent, particularly in the former German territories in China, including Shandong and Tsingtao, which had been seized and still held. In 1914, at Britain's request, Japan had deployed its forces to seize German territories in the Pacific and China, thereby denying them from being used as resupply bases for German forces operating across the region. After the end of the war, Japanese forces remained in China and Korea and by 1931, after seventeen years of military occupation Japan was reluctant to relinquish its position where it now had almost 200,000 troops in 17 divisions based to control the region with its mineral resources. In August 1931, in an overt act of aggression, Japanese troops attacked Manchuria, seizing the Kwantung region with its rich mineral reserves of coal and iron. The following year Japan instigated further incidents against China when the city of Shanghai was bombed. A lack of response by the League of Nations gave Japan the confidence to extend deeper into northern China. By 1937 the size of the military presence doubled and there were incidents along the border with Russia, such as the fighting around Khalkin Gol between May and September 1939.

In September 1937, Japanese troops landed on the Chinese coast north of Shanghai. The Japanese army used convoys of trucks, captured trains and the humble bicycle to transport the troops and supplies to maintain their advance. It has been estimated that during its campaign in China, which lasted between 1937 and 1945, the Japanese army used some 50,000 bicycles.

With the continued rise of militarism across the islands of Japan, students were being encouraged, indeed expected, to join a military organization. Thousands enlisted in the ranks of these groups and were issued with a uniform and other basic equipment, which often included a bicycle. These students would become the future recruits for the army, navy and air force when Japan went to war against the Allies in December 1941.

One country which was keeping itself busy developing new military tactics and units through the early 1930s was Soviet Russia. One of its ideas was to create an airborne force which could be delivered into battle by parachute. In early 1932 the Russians conducted trials to deploy troops by means of parachute near Siverskaya in northern Russia, using a German-designed JuG-1 aircraft. It was realised that once on the ground the lightly armed parachute troops, being without transport, would be vulnerable to attack. Parachute troops were intended to be delivered by air drop very quickly to seize important targets, such as bridges, and the intention was to reinforce them quickly once they had achieved the element of surprise. The Russians realised that if they provided the parachute troops with bicycles they would have transport to move quickly to new positions. The design chosen for the purpose was a model produced by the German company of Opel, which was also making bicycles for the German army. It was a rugged design, capable of withstanding harsh treatment on the battlefield, but it was also light. The Opel bicycles were of the folding design and one type could be used as an extemporised mounting onto which a machine gun could be fitted. However, the idea of fitting a light machine gun to the handlebars of a bicycle proved impractical due to the size and weight of the weapons, just as trials of forty years earlier had shown.

Trials with parachute troops using bicycles continued into the late 1930s, by which time motorbikes and light vehicles were seen as the better option. Even as late as 1941, the Russian army believed a parachute reconnaissance company mounted on bicycles had an operational role, but eventually the idea was abandoned. However, the British 1st and 6th Airborne Divisions, which also included gliders, carried so-called 'parachute bikes' which were really folding bicycles, the design of which went back over forty years.

In 1936 there developed a most aggressive conflict, soon to be known around the world as the Spanish Civil War. The war had been fomenting between Republican troops led by Manuel Azana and Julián Besteiro, who had Communist ideals, opposed by Nationalist forces led by General Francisco Franco, who harboured Fascist ideals. As leaders of Fascist states, Hitler and Mussolini offered to provide military support to General Franco. This elicited a response from Soviet Russia, which as a Communist state announced that it would support the Republicans and pledged to send men, equipment and weapons. Over the next 32 months, between July 1936 and April 1939, each of the warring factions received military support from their respective sponsor countries. Soviet Russia sent shipments of tanks, mostly obsolete, old-fashioned types, as well as other equipment, including weapons. Hitler sent 16,000 German troops to support Franco, along with shipments of modern weapons, tanks and aircraft flown by Luftwaffe pilots. Italy made the greatest contribution to Franco's forces by sending 50,000 troops, aircraft, tanks and artillery along with thousands of tons of ammunition, weapons and other supplies. The war also attracted volunteers from France, Britain, the Republic of Ireland and America.

The arrival of these troops caused problems, not the least of which was the language barrier, and many had little or no military experience. There was also the problem of transportation, because there was not always enough trucks to carry them. To overcome the shortage, bicycles were commandeered from any source available, including from civilians. Factories producing bicycles became important to one side or the other, such as Rabassa, based in Barcelona, which had been manufacturing bicycles since 1922. During the Civil War there was no bicycle production at the factory, but the facilities were taken over by Republican forces which used the resources to repair weapons and to service and maintain vehicles and aircraft engines.

Two other bicycle manufacturing companies, Orbea and Beistegui Hermanos, founded in 1880 and 1909, were both originally manufacturers of small arms, such as the Ruby revolver and rifles. After the end of the First World War, demand for firearms dropped and each of the companies decided separately to diversify into bicycle manufacturing. The company of Orbea employed over 1,000 people and was producing 50,000 bicycles annually. In the early stages of the war the Republican army had some forty infantry regiments, including eight mortar battalions, two machine gun battalions and one battalion mounted on bicycles. Throughout the Spanish Civil War bicycles never made any great impact on the outcome, but the machines did serve the useful purpose of providing a cheap and simple means of transportation.

On 12 March 1938 German troops crossed the border into Austria. Columns of troops marched, while others rode in vehicles or on horses, and further units rode on bicycles to complete the Anschluss, a move which annexed the country to create the 'Greater German Reich'. One of the leading armaments manufacturers in Austria was Steyr which had been established in 1894 for the production of bicycles but by 1938 had diversified into the production of rifles, pistols and machine guns.

Six months later, on 30 September, German troops annexed an area of neighbouring Czechoslovakia along the border between the two countries, and on 15 March 1939, Hitler annexed the rest of Czechoslovakia. The move gave Germany access to more armaments manufacturing such as the important Brno and Praga factories which produced weapons. There was also the Skoda Works, which had been established in 1895 as a bicycle manufacturer before branching into motorcycle production. By 1905 the company was producing vehicles and it was this facility which the German military seized on with relish. Hitler could hardly believe his good fortune when there was no reaction to his latest move. Germany could now benefit from the acquisition of the CKD (Praga) factory which produced armoured vehicles and tanks, and EsKa which had been manufacturing bicycles, which had turned out 21,000 machines in 1914.

In 1939 the German army comprised 51 divisions, of which 39 were infantry, five tank divisions, four light infantry divisions and three mountain divisions. Each had a manpower level of some 18,000 troops. To move this number of troops an infantry division had 1,000 vehicles with

5,400 horses to draw artillery and a fleet of wagons to transport supplies and ammunition. European armies at this time relied on a combination of motorised vehicles, horses and bicycles to provide transport. In fact horses would remain the most widely used mode of transportation throughout the European war and the war in Russia. For example, when Hitler invaded Russia in June 1944, the German army of three million men was supported by 750,000 horses. The Polish army in 1939 had over 80,000 horses in its composition, the Greek army had 125,000 horses and mules, while the Russian Red Army had 1.2 million horses in 1941.

In 1939 the US army consisted of 174,000 men making it smaller than the Portuguese army and barely a quarter the size of the Belgian army, ranking it 18th in the world. In response to the growing tension the military expanded its size to reach 1.4 million men by 1941. The US Army had long showed a preference for motorised transport, but that did not prevent it from considering the purchase of 20,000 horses in 1941.

Bicycles would not be used by the US army in combat. America would fight the war with petrol-driven vehicles, from motorcycles to trucks and tanks, as it had done during the First World War. The purpose of bicycles in the US army was 'To provide transportation for personnel engaged in dispatch or messenger service'. Before October 1942 the bicycles in service in the US army were non-standard 'Bicycle, Military Universal'. They had been adopted by the Ordnance Department and were the military version of the Columbia Model produced by Westfield, which also produced a folding version, the M306, also known as the 'Compax', for use by female personnel serving in the Women's Auxiliary Corps.

In 1942, following America's entry into the war, the country's bicycle production was set at 750,000 machines known as 'Victory' bicycles, produced by twelve factories. But by 1943 only 93,000 machines had been produced for both military and civilian use. Beyond using bicycles for transport on air bases and army camps, the machines had no practical role in combat as far as the US military was concerned. The US Marine Corps trialled bicycles but could not see any serviceable use for them and dropped the whole idea. When the US Army raised airborne divisions, to emulate first the German *Fallschirmjäger* and then the British 1st and 6th Airborne Divisions, it was proposed to equip them with folding bicycles to provide a means of transport when on the ground. It was based on the

When the Americans began to arrive in Britain by 1942 many personnel used bicycles to move around their bases.

German infantry on bicycles formed part of the Blitzkrieg into Poland in 1939 and again during the attack on France in 1940.

Infantry on bicycles during the Blitzkriegs in 1939 and 1940.

premise that infantry marching could cover around 25 miles in 24 hours but a man on a bicycle could cover three times that distance. However, that estimate was based on peacetime military exercises under known controlled conditions. In reality such estimates were shown to be overly optimistic. During a battle, when an enemy is shooting, it is impossible to ride a bicycle normally and road conditions will not always be suitable. Exactly how much the use of the bicycle would be reduced under actual combat conditions would be shown during the D-Day landings on 6 June 1944 and the subsequent campaign to liberate Europe.

In 1939 a typical infantry division of the German army contained a reconnaissance *Abteilung* (section). The divisional reconnaissance *Abteilung* included a mounted squadron, a bicycle squadron and a 'heavy' squadron. At regimental headquarters level, each had a signals platoon with bicycle troops, meaning that there were 39 infantry divisional bicycle squadrons and further 117 regimental headquarters each with bicycle troops. These troops used the *Truppenfahrrad* (German Army Bicycle) and were organised into units known as *Radfahrbeweglichemarschgruppe* (Mobile Bicycle March Groups). In September 1939 a company in a typical *Radfahrerschwadron*, Cavalry Bicycle Squadron, had 138 bicycles to equip three rifle squads each with at least twelve men armed with machine guns and rifles. The headquarters section included three messengers and an NCO section leader each on bicycles and the medic section had five men on bicycles also. To support and service the machines the company had three bicycle mechanics with equipment carried in several trucks.

Other units of the German army to be issued with bicycles included specialist troops such as the *Gebirgsjäger* mountain troops. On the outbreak of war there were three mountain divisions, each with a typical manpower level of 14,000 of all ranks and operational roles. For example, in each division there were two infantry regiments with 6,500 men including engineers, artillery and signals battalion, along with a cycle battalion included in the formation with a manpower level of 550 men. They were equipped with the regulation bicycle, fitted with brackets to carry weapons, including machine guns and the 5cm calibre *Granatewerfer* 36 light mortar. The *Gebirgsjäger* units fought in mountainous terrain, such as the Tatra and Carpathian Mountains, Norway, Balkans, Crete, the Alps in northern Italy and the Vosges in France. The bicycles were intended to serve in the role of reconnaissance and liaison duties, but in mountain conditions their use was limited. Horses were more useful in such circumstances.

There were many factories producing bicycles for the German army, the leading companies being Torpedo, Phanomen, Solinger-Fahrradwerke, Adler Werke, and Opel. In February 1937 Opel halted production of bicycles to concentrate on motor vehicles for the German army. During its time as a bicycle manufacturer it had produced over 2.6 million machines, many of which were used by the German army in both world wars. But production of bicycles was not overly affected by the departure of Opel. In 1943 German factories turned out 1.2 million bicycles with more produced by factories in the occupied countries, especially Czechoslovakia and France.

The *Bund Deutscher Mädel* (the women's branch of the Hitler Youth Movement) and the *Reichsarbeitsdienst* (Reich Labour Corps) or RAD, which was a workforce used to clear away rubble and repair damage after air raids, also made extensive use of bicycles which could transport their tools, such as spades and pickaxes, in place of rifles. Members of this organization were also given military training and as the war developed they were involved in fighting, especially in the defence of Berlin during the final months of the war.

On 1 September 1939, Hitler ordered an attack against Poland. To face this attack, the Polish army had approximately 1.5 million men, 10,000 pieces of artillery including anti-tank and anti-aircraft guns, and 1,000 armoured vehicles. The Polish army also deployed 210 squadrons of cavalry forces, some of which, incredibly, still rode horses and used sabres in battle. Cavalry brigades were intended to provide support to the infantry along with bicycle-mounted troops. The Polish bicycle companies each contained 196 bicycles and horse-drawn wagons within the infantry regiments making up a division. These companies would be divided into platoons, each with around fifty cyclists. They were equipped with the 'Typ Wojskowy' (Army Type) Model 35 produced by the company of Radom. The Polish army had 100,000 such machines in service before 1939.

A generation earlier, in 1920, Polish soldiers had fought for independence against Russia. At that time the members of the Warsaw Cycling Association had played a part in the fighting by acting as messengers to deliver orders between units. They were formed into groups of about 120 and could serve as infantry just as the British Army Cyclist Corps had done in France and Belgium. A Polish officer of the time noted how, in his opinion, the role of an army cyclist was to be 'swiftly riding infantry capable of conducting intense fire combat. Therefore, their natural purpose is to reinforce and collaborate with cavalry units, because they have the very qualities cavalry lacks.' He meant, of course, that they made less noise and had a reduced silhouette.

On the second day of the invasion, elements of the German XIX Corps, commanded by General Heinz Guderian, encountered Polish troops defending the approaches to the Brahe River preventing a crossing from being made. Living up to his nickname of 'Fast Heinz', Guderian went forward to personally sort out the problem. He organised rubber boats to cross the troops, which on reaching the opposite bank captured a company of cyclist troops who were holding the position.

The Polish army secured minor victories such as the engagement around the town of Krasnobród on 23 September 1939, involving the 2nd Commonwealth Cavalry attached as part of the 25th Greater Poland Uhlan Regiment. As a platoon of cyclists were advancing they changed direction and began to move towards the village of Podklasztor, which lay about one mile away and from where the Polish Uhlans had just withdrawn, leaving the Germans in control. As the Polish troops extended to attack, their platoon commander, Lieutenant Srutka, was killed. His was replaced by Misionko who took over control of the platoon and led it into the attack. A squadron of Polish cavalry charged using sabres to chase out the Germans who came under fire from the cyclist troops. The action had been brief but 47 Germans were killed, 30 wounded and 100 taken prisoner. Polish losses were 26 killed and 35 wounded.

The Polish surrendered on 27 September and anything deemed to be of use was pressed into service by both the German and Russian armies, including bicycles.

As surprising as the Polish campaign had been, it was what happened next that shook the world. On 30 November, only eight weeks after the surrender of the Polish Army to the Russians, Stalin ordered an attack against Finland. The most likely reason for this was to seize Finland's nickel mines, valuable for the production of armour plate. The Russo-Finnish War of 1939–40, or 'Winter War' as it was also known lasted almost four months and by the time it ended on 13 March 1940 the Finnish army had killed or wounded some 200,000 Russians and destroyed 1,600 tanks, in return for which the Red Army had killed 25,000 Finnish soldiers. The winter conditions with sub-zero temperatures, icy roads and deep snow drifts prevented the use of ordinary wheeled vehicles, and even tanks with their tracks could not operate to their fullest capacity. Bicycles, which were used by troops on both sides, could not operate, leaving them to fight as dismounted infantry.

On 25 June 1941, only three days after Hitler attacked Russia, Finland allied itself with Germany. The Finnish army mobilised 400,000 troops, later rising to 650,000, in what would be referred to as the 'War of Continuation'. In the intervening fifteen months, Finland had reorganised the army and re-equipped with weapons and vehicles, which included bicycle troops.

In June 1944 the Finns took up positions on the Karelian Isthmus, a land mass measuring about fifty miles across. The Karelian Front, because of the way in which the defensive lines had been constructed, extended some 130 miles. In charge of defending the city of Vyborg was General Govorov, initially with 270,000 troops supported by 620 tanks, 1,660 pieces of artillery and 1,500 aircraft. Across the front itself there were another 184,000 troops supported by more than 1,200 pieces of artillery and 363 tanks. Even holding static lines against such strong defences the Finnish positions were not sufficient for a prolonged siege. Nevertheless, they held the lines to cut off the city from outside support. Patrols were conducted to probe Russian defences and limited actions were undertaken during which Finnish troops captured supplies and weapons. In the warm summer months the network of unmade roads between villages and towns were firm enough for Finnish troops on bicycles to use them as transportation routes. These included light detachments of Jaeger Companies from the Jaeger Battalions. They used the models produced by either the factory of Tenturi or Monark. The Finns proved themselves to be very adept at moving very quickly and undetected, such as the Pori Brigade whose troops used bicycles for mobility and to transport supplies for these patrols. The Pori Brigade dated back to the Thirty Years War and had served in various wars including the Civil War of 1918 which gave Finland its independence from Russia.

The Jaeger Companies mounted on bicycles proved highly effective in 'hit and run' guerrilla-type operations against the Russians. The 1st Jaeger Brigade was equipped with both tank and anti-tank battalions, with the infantry being mounted on bicycles for mobility when conditions allowed. During the winter months these troops would convert to become ski troops, still being mobile to operate as infantry. As the war developed, the Finnish army formed special fighting units to engage in anti-tank tactics. One of these specialist units was the 'Taisteluosasto Puroma' (Battlegroup Puromo) named after the unit's commander, Colonel Albert Puroma. Formed in February 1944 by the highly decorated officer it was one of the leading units which made up part of the infantry portion of the Finnish Armoured Division, which included the 1st Jaeger Brigade with a combined force of more than 3,000 infantry in three battalions equipped with bicycles. They proved themselves very capable and took part in counter-attack actions, such as that mounted against Russian forces near the town of Kuuterselka on the evening of 14 February 1944. The ensuing battle was a hard-fought contest with the Finnish infantry supporting their armour during the attack. The fighting continued through the following day and although they inflicted heavy losses, the Russians had superiority in numbers of troops and tanks. The Finns sustained severe losses, especially the Finnish Armoured Division. Battlegroup Puroma was forced to withdraw and take up new positions, having suffered 627 casualties. Several months later, on 15 September 1944, Finland signed an Armistice with Russia. The Finnish army now pursued the German army back to Norway, during which the bicycle troops of the Jaeger Brigade spearheaded the Finnish advance through Lapland.

On 9 April 1940, Hitler launched a combined naval and airborne operation against neutral Denmark. The tiny standing Danish army numbered around 10,000 men. It included bicycle troops. The Guard Hussar Regiment of the 1st Zealand Division contained a cyclist squadron with several units including a medium machine gun squadron. The Jutland Dragoon Regiment of the 2nd Jutland Division also contained cyclist units. However, the small Danish force was soon overwhelmed and surrendered on the same day.

On the same day Germany attacked Denmark, German troops also attacked Norway, taking the fighting to the borders of neutral Sweden.

The Norwegian army had a mobilised strength of 100,000 men, equipped with mainly old-fashioned weapons and equipment, including horse-drawn artillery. An infantry regiment had a manpower level of 3,750 troops and within this structure there were companies equipped with bicycles for reconnaissance duties. The Dragoon Regiment was another unit containing bicycle troops, having three squadrons of bicycles in its 'Wheeled Section' whose troops would fight as dismounted infantry. The bicycles could only be used during the short spring and summer period when there was no snow. During the winter months these troops, like the Finnish army, left their bicycles in storage to take to skis.

German parachute troops captured Oslo on 9 April and further landings by airborne troops took place at Stavanger and Dombas, where fighting broke out. The initial assault had been fast but bad weather delayed reinforcements from arriving as fast. Nevertheless, the speed of the German attack and the troops with their better training and equipment gained the upper hand. Infantry landed at Oslo from troopships where they took to their bicycles and advanced inland rapidly to seize installations and bridges. British and French troops arrived in Norway at the beginning of May but their presence only served to prolong the fighting which, from the start, was always going to go in Germany's favour. The campaign lasted two months during which time the Norwegians had no time to use their cyclist troops, not that they could have achieved much against troops with modern weapons and equipment.

Chapter 10

Wheels Turn West: Blitzkrieg 1940

When Hitler launched the attack westward against Belgium, Holland and France, codenamed 'Fall Gelb' (Case Yellow) on 10 May 1940, the German army unleased the full weight of Blitzkrieg, a strategy of combined forces using tactics never before encountered by western European armies. The method of attack had been used against Poland but the campaign ended before it could be fully put to practice. Advancing on a broad front with plenty of scope for manoeuvre the German army could show what modern warfare was like. Blitzkrieg (Lightning War) relied on speed and weight of numbers brought to bear along a line of advance without deviation. It was an all arms tactic using infantry supported by artillery and armour, which in turn was supported by aircraft to attack strategic points.

Holland, as a neutral state, had not been engaged in a war for over 140 years. The country maintained a status of armed neutrality, and the Dutch army could not have been any less prepared for an attack than were the Poles in September 1939. When Germany attacked on 10 May 1940, the Dutch army only managed to resist for five days. At the time of the attack the Dutch army had a nucleus of 1,500 professional officers and 6,500 other regulars of all ranks. It was this small force which was responsible for training the annual intake of some 60,000 conscripts which made up the bulk of the standing army. On mobilisation the Dutch army had 270,000 troops with a call-up of all reserve forces.

In May 1940 the Dutch army, like other European armies, relied on bicycles to provide transportation for individuals, having as many as 150,000 machines in service. Around 65,000 men in four divisions, almost 25 per cent of the total force available to the defence of the country, were ordered to deploy and take up positions on the left wing of the defensive position known as the Grebbe Line, which extended for 25 miles and comprised trenches and pillboxes.

Recreated Dutch army cyclists showing how the troops looked in 1940 when attacked by Germany in 1940.

The Dutch army had not fought a war for 140 years and was not prepared for Blitzkrieg.

At infantry brigade level HQs had cyclist troops serving as messengers, and with very few radios sets for communication these cyclists were kept very busy. The Light Division had 1st and 2nd Wielrijders (Bicycle) Regiments within a division, with each battalion having three companies equipped with bicycles. Four of the Hussars Regiments each had four squadrons of troops mounted on bicycles.

After five days of action on the ground and being pounded by air raids, the Dutch government surrendered on 14 May. The total casualty list for the Dutch army was 2,332 killed and several thousand wounded. After the campaign Hitler wrote: 'They put up a much stronger resistance than we expected. Many of their units fought very bravely. But they had neither appropriate training nor experience of war. For this reason they were usually overcome by German forces which were often numerically very inferior.'

The Belgian army was larger and had some better weaponry and vehicles. In the end it fared little better than the Dutch, but it did manage to withstand the German attack for longer. At the same time as Belgium surrendered on 27 May, the BEF and French troops were fighting a rearguard action to cover the withdrawal to Dunkirk.

Belgium reverted to its declared state of neutrality at the end of the First World War and now, like its Dutch neighbour, had repeated its neutral status when hostilities broke out in 1939. The country retained an army with a peacetime strength of 100,000 men which could be increased to 650,000 on mobilisation, a figure which included 150,000 reservists. The army was composed of nine corps, seven of which were infantry, being divided to cover three corps areas, including Antwerp, Brussels and Liege, while three independent frontier bicycle battalions were deployed along the border with six infantry divisions and two cavalry divisions to provide armoured support. Corps were sub-divided into divisions, each of which had three brigades in a structure known as 'triangular' from everything being formed in threes, including the brigades which were composed of three battalions. The Belgian army employed bicycles to a greater degree than any of the other Allied armies, using them at all levels from battalion strength up to a complete company at Divisional HQ level, including a bicycle pioneer battalion to undertake engineering tasks, including such roles as destroying bridges to hamper the enemy's advance. The army even had a specialist unit, the Chasseurs Ardennais Division, which was comprised almost entirely of cyclist troops who were used in reconnaissance roles and messenger duties. The unit had three independent bicycle battalions, each with three companies, to form a brigade-size unit serving as frontier guards.

The Belgian army had been in contact with the German army for several months throughout the period of the Phoney War, when men from the Chasseurs Ardennais, also known as the Cyclistes Frontières de Limbourg, patrolled the border with Germany. During this period of inactivity sentries on both sides began to fraternise with one another. For the Germans it was probably a means of relieving the tedious monotony of sentry duty. For the Belgians, there was an ulterior motive behind their display of amiability. The reconnaissance officers of the Chasseur Ardennaise hoped to gain information from the German guards which might give an indication of Germany's intentions. For weeks nothing was forthcoming until on 9 May the German guards' attitude changed. While not entirely hostile, they instructed the Belgian guards to keep their distance. As the day wore on German attitude became more abrupt and vehicle movement increased.

As night fell, vehicle lights could be seen moving and the sound of engine noise increased. Shouting could be heard and just after 11 pm reconnaissance officers from the Chasseur Ardennaise passed on this news to General Raoul van Overstraeten, the military adviser to King Leopold, warning that an attack was impending. The orders he passed on to local commanders were not all heeded at first, but by 1.30 am on the morning of 10 May, units along the border were going on the alert. At 4 am the first German aircraft were seen flying westwards and gliders landed at Eben Emael where airborne troops neutralised the defences. All along the border German troops now advanced towards Holland, Belgium and France further south.

Four months earlier, 10 January 1940, around mid-day, two non-commissioned officers, Sergeant Frans Habets and Corporal Gerard Rubens, from the Chasseurs Ardennaise, while riding bicycles on patrol from Vucht, just south of Eisden, to investigate an aircraft crashed near Mechelen-sur-Meuse, about two miles distant, became involved in an incident which could have revealed more about the Germans' intentions than the Belgian army could ever have dared hope. The episode began earlier in the morning when Major Erich Hoenmanns, piloting a Messerschmitt Bf 108 'Taifun' (Typhoon) aircraft took off from Loddenheide to fly to Cologne about 100 miles to the south. Weather conditions were snow and ice, but nothing to prevent take-off with his passenger, Major Helmuth Reinberger, on board. It was not long into the flight when Hoenmanns became disorientated and couldn't identify any landmark to give him his location. He chose to fly west, and not long after, power to the engine was lost. Looking for somewhere to land, Hoenmanns decided to put down in a field, but as he was descending he struck trees causing severe damage to the aircraft. The two men were badly shaken but otherwise unhurt. Major Reinberger moved to a sheltered position out of the wind, opened his briefcase and began to set fire to the documents inside. At that point, Habets and Rubens appeared on their bicycles, identifying the men as German from the markings on the aircraft and, seeing the documents being burned, realised that the situation was suspicious and reacted quickly. The burning documents were extinguished and saved.

During questioning, both men revealed their rank and names. Major Reinberger identified himself as being on the staff of Fliegerfuhrer 220 responsible for supplying Fliegerdivision 7 during combat operations. Over the next few days the Belgians managed to piece together something of the documents, the importance of which was now becoming clear, although certain questions remained unanswered. Why was Reinberger travelling with highly classified documents? Secondly, why did Hoenmanns head west towards Belgium? The only conclusion they could reach was that both men were traitors, working in unison to present the documents to the Allies. Fortunately for the Germans, the Belgians were not in possession of all the facts because most of the documents had been burned. Had they had the complete document they would have learned of Hitler's intention to attack on 14 January. General Van Overstraeten thought the documents were a hoax, but British and French moved troops close to the Belgian border just in case Germany did attack. Belgium could not risk violating its own neutrality by allowing Germany's enemy onto its soil and give Hitler a reason to attack.

The original German plan had called for the army to attack Belgium's north-east border. Hitler, realising the original plan was now compromised, knew that a new plan would have to be devised. Now, four months after the so-called 'Mechelen Affair', this new plan was put into operation. The attack against Belgium's north-east border was still implemented with 3rd and 4th Panzer Divisions advancing to the River Dyle. Further to the south, three Panzer Divisions forced their way through the densely-wooded region of the Ardennes, a route which no military planner on the Allied side expected. After two days of fighting the French 2nd and 9th Armies were falling back. As for Major Reinberger and Major Hoenmanns, as prisoners of war, they were removed to England and survived the war.

The idea for the creation of a Belgian bicycle force to patrol the border region with Germany was first proposed by Colonel Bremer in 1914. With the outbreak of war that year nothing further was done and by 1918 the suggestion had all but been forgotten. In 1928 the idea was resurrected by General Hellebaut. This time it was acted on and the first elements of the new Frontier Cyclists unit were formed for the specific role of border patrol. Five years later, in March 1933, King Albert I gave the unit the name Chasseurs Ardennais and by March 1937 it had expanded to three regiments, with the first being located at Arlon, the second at Bastogne and the third at Vielsalm. Each comprised three battalions with three companies of cyclists armed with rifles and machine guns. For support they could rely on light tanks, anti-tank guns and motorcycle combinations. When Britain and France declared war on Germany the strength of the unit was greatly increased.

Cyclist troops were engaged in regular border patrols on the night of 9/10 May 1940 in a heightened state of readiness. At around 3.30 am movement and noise alerted the Belgians that the Germans were going to attack. Platoons and companies were now being dispatched to cover bridges across the waterways crisscrossing the region. A company was sent to Gruitrode at around 7 am and another to Lommel at 8 am. Another company was sent to the Lanklaar Bridge, which was being used as a staging area for troops to gather for deployment.

Around midnight of 9/10 May two cyclist companies were on a high state of alert at the Briegden-Neerharen link channel which connects the Albert Canal to the South William Canal. Belgian engineers had instructions to prepare the bridges for demolition and bicycle troops had been deployed across the area to bridges across the waterways. The bridge at Vroenhoven, which was being defended by Sergeant Crauwels with bicycle troops, was captured after a fierce exchange of fire in which the Belgians suffered several losses.

The following day, 11 May, around 3.50 am, the Germans maintained the pressure of their advance along the border, bringing pressure to bear on the Belgians at Tongres. The Limburg Border Cyclist Battalion which was defending the area around Kleine-Spouwen was joined by other cyclist troops defending designated positions. For the next ten days the border cyclist units of the Chasseurs Ardennais conducted a fighting withdrawal as dismounted infantry, along with other elements of the Belgian army, using their bicycles as transport. Always in danger of running out of supplies, the troops were fed by the local populace. Lack of ammunition was a problem. On 21 May, Lieutenant Colonel De Loucker, the corps chief of the 44th Line Regiment, ordered the border cyclists to the Zwijnaarde Bridge to take up position throughout the morning. Artillery and aerial bombardment caused heavy casualties and the position was evacuated around 2.30 pm.

At around 3 pm on 26 May, the remnants of the Limburg Border Cyclist Battalion arrived at Kachtem. One troop had five officers, three NCOs and seven men, while another, lacking officers, had four NCOs and eighteen soldiers. By the end of the day a further 200 Chasseur Ardennais border cyclists had arrived at Kachtem. The troops were given little time to rest before being ordered to move north-west towards the town of Gits, about nine miles away. On 28 May news was beginning to circulate that the Belgian government had surrendered. The troops were assembled to be told officially the news of the surrender. The survivors were directed to make their way to Olsene, where the last to arrive two days later, having ridden their bicycles, were ordered to surrender to the Germans and hand over their weapons and bicycles. The bicycle troops had fought bravely throughout the campaign and probably suffered the most casualties out of any Belgian unit committed to the fight.

For eighteen days the troops had fought to the best of their ability. Hitler composed an assessment of the Belgian soldier: 'generally fought very bravely. His experience of war was considerably greater than the Dutch. At the beginning his tenacity was astonishing... This is now decreasing visibly as the Belgian soldier realises that his basic function is to cover the British retreat.' Rommel, in a reference to the Belgians' green uniform, said of them: 'They are not men, they are green wolves.'

Things were not going well for the BEF. On 18 May 1940, Major Arthur West serving with the 5th Battalion the Buffs at the French town of Doullens, where 36 Brigade attached to 12 Division had taken up defensive positions, witnessed columns of refugees streaming west along with retreating French soldiers: 'Some rode bicycles gathered on the way, or drove farm wagons. Others rode horses.' When motor vehicles ran out of fuel they were abandoned, clogging the already overcrowded roads even further and slowing down the passage of those walking. Those refugees riding bicycles were the lucky ones. Bicycles were being ridden by soldiers and civilians alike; it was not always easy to differentiate between the two, and who was friendly and who was enemy. At Berchem, where the Northamptonshire Regiment was holding defensive positions during the retreat to Dunkirk, sentries observed: 'At about 11 am a group of about twelve apparent refugees approached. To Captain Hart it seemed that they were walking with a somewhat martial stride and his suspicions were confirmed when they were followed by about twenty cyclists, riding in pairs, and a lorry. The section covering the road held their fire until the cyclists were a good target at close range and opened fire with Bren and rifles.' Erring on the side of caution to prevent an unfortunate accident in killing one's own side could prove to be a fatal mistake. In this instance, it had been a close thing but turned out to be the right decision.

On 23 May as the British were falling back towards Furnes, a guardsman of 1st Battalion Grenadier Guards observed 'about a mile away and out of range… a party of Germans [who] could be seen marching and wheeling bicycles at about the same speed.' Both the Germans and Grenadiers arrived in Furnes at about the same time where there was fierce exchange of fire, which ended with the Guards falling back to La Panne about four miles north-west of Furnes.

Three days later, news was circulated that a general order for all troops to evacuate to Dunkirk was issued. On that day B Company of the 4th Royal Sussex Regiment was holding positions around Caestre, where two men from the company were assigned to undertake observation duties, for which task they were issued with 'binoculars, a bike, paper and pencil.' They remained in place, observing passing traffic, mainly refugees, reporting back to battalion HQ at regular intervals. When German tanks appeared they knew it was time to leave.

The British army was well equipped with motor transport, but there remained a role for bicycles in some units. In 1939 each battalion HQ had three bicycles which increased to six machines by 1943. The signals platoon within a battalion also had at least eight bicycles which could be used for liaison and delivering messages.

Between 26 May and 4 June 338,000 men were evacuated from the beaches around Dunkirk, 139,000 of which were French and Belgian troops. The BEF left behind 68,111 men killed, wounded, missing and taken prisoner. They had lost 2,472 pieces of artillery, 63,879 motor vehicles and 20,548 motorcycles. Out of a force of some 700 armoured vehicles sent to France only 25 were brought back.

The French government surrendered to the Germans on 21 June, by which time the campaign had cost the French army 90,000 killed and 200,000 wounded, with the remainder of the army, around 1.9 million men, capitulating seventeen days after the Dunkirk evacuation. The

After Dunkirk the British army had to rearm and re-equip with weapons, vehicles and even bicycles.

surrendering French troops were disarmed and taken into captivity and all their remaining weapons, vehicles and equipment were taken into German service.

All the armies engaged in the European campaign had used bicycles, and while not vital during the campaign they had proved useful. The bicycles which had been used by the French, Belgian, Dutch and British armies now provided the German army with a cheap and easy means to patrol its newly won territories. The fact that workers still had to travel to their place of employment or to buy food was of no concern to the Germans, who added to the problem by commandeering bicycles from civilians. This caused a shortage of bicycles which, as the war went on, became an important mode of transport for everyday life.

This fact was highlighted in January 1945 when a conversation was overheard between two German prisoners of war. The first prisoner confided to his colleague that he had shot a French civilian he had seen riding a bicycle. On being asked if he believed the Frenchman posed a threat, the first man replied in a very matter of fact manner that he only wanted the bicycle.

In June 1940, just before the Germans arrived on the Channel Islands to begin almost five long years of occupation, the States (local government) on Jersey sought to curb the movement of enemy aliens on the island. A curfew was implemented on aliens aged between 16 and 60. There were just sixteen such 'enemy aliens' on the island, and the States forbade them to possess or borrow bicycles.

In 1941 the German military began to implement occupation measures in the Channel Islands, including fuel rationing. The Feldkommandant issued orders that the military government was to requisition bicycles, citing Article 53 of the Hague Convention. All protestations from the States were ignored by the Germans. Indeed, when Guernsey failed to supply the set number of bicycles the *Nebenstelle* threatened action against the President of the Controlling Committee, accusing him of 'intolerable sabotage' which would result in imprisonment. This threat produced results and all demands for bicycles were met. Children were told to walk to school rather than ride bicycles. People who required the machines to go to work were told the same. Even doctors were not exempt. It became an offence for civilians to buy or sell bicycles, punishable by imprisonment, but that did not prevent them from being traded for goods or even sold, fetching prices of over £40 on Jersey. In the first months of the occupation bicycles were being sold on Guernsey for £5 and within two years that price had risen to £50. With few padlocks, theft of unattended bicycles was prevented by the simple expedient of removing the saddle.

In France, Belgium and Holland, resistance movements were formed. They were supported by the Allies who delivered arms and equipment to them. To move around, the resistance fighters could blend in by using public transport such as trains and buses. At a meeting between two Dutch resistance fighters in Winterswijk, one offered his female opposite number advice that could save her life: 'The places where I go, I meet people and I go there by bicycle, but I don't dare travel by train.' In Amsterdam, resistance fighters used bicycles to smuggle Jews out of the city to prevent the Germans taking them to concentration camps. It was too dangerous to use motor vehicles. Bicycles were frequently used to deliver messages. Resistance fighters hid messages inside the hollow tubes of the frame. These operations were vital to the Allies in planning the invasion of France. After the Normandy landings bicycles continued to be used by resistance groups conducting operations against the Germans as they retreated eastwards.

The SAS, formed in 1941, was considered perfect to work with the French Resistance in the Normandy Campaign. On 6/7 June 1944, forty men from 'B' Squadron of 1st SAS were parachuted into France to undertake Operation Bulbasket. Together with local Resistance groups they were to destroy railway tracks and bridges to hamper the movement of the Germans. The SAS set up their base in the forest of Verrières in the Viene and it was to here that the Resistance brought news concerning the rail junction at Châtellerault, where the Germans had a huge stock of fuel and other supplies. Commanding the operation was Captain John Tonkin, who deputed Lieutenant Tomos (Twm) Stephens to scout the target in preparation for attack. Stephens, wearing civilian clothes, accompanied by two Frenchmen acting as guides, rode bicycles to the target area thirty miles away. Stephens saw that the size of the stockpile of eleven full trains with fuel was not an exaggeration by excitable Frenchmen. The small group retraced their route on their bicycles back to Verrières. They had been away for 36 hours, having ridden their bicycles

70 miles in the round trip. Stephens made his report to Captain Tonkin who told the radio operator to send a message to London with all the details. Three hours later, twenty-four Mosquito bombers attacked the junction at Châtellerault and destroyed the site. This successful outcome had been made possible by use of bicycles. The SAS relocated their base but returned to their original site which had been compromised. On 4 July the base was attacked and a fierce firefight ensued. The surviving SAS were captured and later executed under the directions of Hitler's notorious 'Commando Order'.

Perhaps the most famous operation in which resistance fighters used bicycles was 'Operation Anthropoid', the assassination of Reinhard Heydrich, the appointed Protector of Moravia and Bohemia, the title given to Czechoslovakia by the Germans. It was decided by the Czechoslovak Government in exile, led by Eduard Beneš, that Heydrich should be assassinated. A small group of volunteer Czechoslovak soldiers serving in exile were trained by the SOE for the mission. In December 1941 the group of nine men were parachuted into Czechoslovakia. Over the next five months they planned the mission, for which they were helped by Prague locals using bicycles to reconnoitre possible locations suitable to ambush Heydrich, deliver information and pass messages.

On 27 May 1942 the opportunity presented itself and Jozef Gabčik and Jan Kubiš threw hand grenades at Heydrich's car as it passed their position on the road. Heydrich later died of his wounds. The Germans gathered information and items left at the scene, which included bicycles used as transport by the two men. These were displayed and details circulated in the press to elicit information from the public. The SOE group was finally traced to their hiding place in a crypt beneath the church of Saints Cyril and Methodius in Prague. A firefight ended with the deaths of all the men in the church.

These are just two notable examples, but bicycles were instrumental in the success of many missions undertaken by resistance groups in all occupied countries.

Chapter 11

Hitler's Allies

Finland became an ally of Germany in 1941 following Hitler's attack on Soviet Russia. The Finnish army made extensive use of bicycles, including a rifle battalion mounted on bicycles within the Independent Cavalry Brigade.

In November 1940, Romania became a not-wholly-willing ally of Germany, which reorganised and re-equipped the Romanian army. Two years later it had expanded to 250,000 men, which was committed to supporting Germany in the campaign in Russia. Each division of the Romanian army included a reconnaissance battalion equipped with bicycles.

Another of Germany's allies was Hungary which deployed troops to the Eastern Front as early as July 1941. The Hungarian army included a special unit called the 'Rapid' Corps. Despite this name it relied on horses and bicycles for transportation. These bicycle formations would discover, like the Finnish and Norwegian armies, that bicycles are no use in snow and icy conditions.

Initially Bulgaria was neutral, but it became a signatory to the Tripartite Pact on 1 March 1941, becoming an ally of Hitler. The country sent troops into Yugoslavia and Greece on 20 April 1941. After Germany's attack on Russia, Bulgarian troops also served on the Eastern Front, mobilising a total of 450,000 men. Modern equipment supplied by Germany replaced otherwise obsolete weaponry and vehicles. The army used a large number of horses and there were bicycles in some units.

Hitler's oldest ally was Mussolini. They shared an association going back to when they supported Franco's Nationalist forces in the Spanish Civil War. Italy would mobilise 4.5 million men who would serve in theatres of war from North Africa to Russia, Greece and Albania, including fighting in Italy itself from 1943 when the Allies invaded. During the course of the war Italy would lose 380,000 killed and 225,000 wounded, along with hundreds of thousands taken prisoner during the campaigns in Russia and North Africa.

In August 1939, Count Galeazzo Ciano, the Italian Foreign Minister and Mussolini's son-in-law, tried to explain to Mussolini that the country was not ready to go to war. Ignoring the advice, Mussolini declared war against France and Britain on 10 June 1940. On 21 June a general attack was launched by thirty-two Italian divisions advancing into the French Alps. The Italian army had its elite units, such as the Bersaglieri and the six specialist Alpini divisions which were trained in mountain warfare. One of the regiments taking part in the campaign was the 4th Bersaglieri within which each of its three battalions had bicycle troops. It was to prove an ill-fated operation, during which the Italians lost more troops to frostbite than through fighting. It revealed how poorly prepared the Italian army was.

At the beginning of the war there were twelve regiments of Bersaglieri, which were mostly motorised but still retained cyclist troops in the HQ company of each of the 850-man battalions. The regiments served in various theatres from Russia to Yugoslavia and Greece as well as serving in Italy. The 28th served with the 101st Motorised Division Trieste, being destroyed in the battle of El Alamein in November 1942. The 18th Bersaglieri saw service in Russia in April 1942, and in the South of France and Italy in 1943.

Chapter 12

Britain Stands Alone

In Britain in 1940 private car ownership was around one vehicle for every fourteen head of population, while some ten million bicycles were owned, representing one machine for every 4.8 people, making it the most widely used means of private transportation, mainly for the factory workers.

When Britain declared war on 3 September 1939, Winston Churchill, serving at the time as the First Lord of the Admiralty, called for a home defence force to be raised. On 13 May the plan to form the Local Defence Volunteers (LDV) was approved and the following evening Antony Eden, as Secretary of State for War, broadcast the news to the nation on the

Factories produced thousands of bicycles for use by the military, for civilians and emergency services.

The Local Defence Volunteer force was a forerunner to the Home Guard in the early months of the war and members used their bicycles to cover a wide area when on patrol.

radio. He appealed for men aged between 17 and 65 years who were not in military service. In the first week, 250,000 volunteered, many of whom had served in former conflicts. On 22 July 1940, the LDV was renamed the Home Guard and this brought a fresh wave of volunteers. At the peak of its strength the Home Guard had almost 1.7 million volunteers. They were equipped with standard and non-standard weapons and equipment, some of which was positively 'Heath Robinson' in design, such as the Blacker Bombard and the Northover Projector.

Members of the Home Guard took their role very seriously and undertook patrols to guard installations such as gas works, bridges, railway lines and power stations, which were deemed vulnerable to attacks of sabotage. Patrols were often conducted on foot, some used boats to patrol waterways and rivers, on Dartmoor and Exmoor the men rode horses, but many rode their own bicycles which allowed them to cover more ground and carry equipment and supplies for extended patrols. Exercises were organised to train the men and test their skills. During these exercises they practised evacuating wounded men using two bicycles secured side by side with a stretcher suspended between them. It was a method used

Home Guard units across the country used bicycles to keep mobile.

Bicycles were used by the Home Guard in town and country.

forty years earlier and was still useful. The configuration provided a stable platform: when the riders dismounted, the bicycles could be left free-standing to allow a medic to treat the man on the stretcher.

There were many other organizations which used bicycles, such as the 14,000 women delivering mail for the Post Office. Across the country

Home Guard units could carry their weapons and supplies for extended patrols.

The Women's Land Army delivered parcels by bicycle.

In remote areas the bicycle was essential to the Women's Land Army for transport.

the police forces, the Red Cross and St John's Ambulance services, the wardens of the Air Raid Precaution, and the Auxiliary Fire Service, all used bicycles at various stages. Many of the 80,000 members of the Women's Land Army and the 6,000 members of the Women's Timber Corps used bicycles.

The Women's Voluntary Service, WVS, had been created by Stella Isaacs in 1938. During the war its members helped rehouse people whose homes had been destroyed in the bombing. In the first months of the war they also assisted with the evacuation of some 1.5 million children from cities to safer homes in the country. Over one million women served in the WVS and although they had access to the car pool scheme, the alternative was to use privately owned bicycles.

Women also went into the armed forces, including 74,635 in the Women's Royal Navy Service (WRNS), 182,000 in the Women's Auxiliary Air Force (WAAF), and 190,000 in the Auxiliary Territorial Service (ATS) serving in a variety of roles including 'mixed' battery anti-aircraft guns. They used their bicycles to deliver messages as dispatch riders around the camps and air bases.

The Girl Guides played their part too, taking to their bicycles to help victims of air raids by rendering first aid and delivering parcels put together by the WVS or WI for those whose houses had been destroyed in the Blitz.

On the 'Home Front', when London, Swansea, Coventry, Bristol, Exeter and Liverpool were targetted by the Luftwaffe, sirens alerted civilians of imminent air raids and to seek safety in the shelters. The instruction was reinforced by police officers on bicycles riding around the streets with placards suspended from their necks with the instruction to 'Take Cover'. Approximately 60,000 police officers served in 182 police forces in the war, in 58 county forces and 122 city and borough forces. The Metropolitan Police Force had 20,000 officers to protect docks against theft and sabotage. By 1944 they were augmented by some 17,000 War Reserve Police and Special Constables, including almost 400 women police officers. Many cyclists, especially air raid wardens, were killed in the war by motorists not used to driving in the blackout conditions.

In 1942, after two years of training the first battalions of airborne forces were ready. Churchill now had the beginnings of what would develop into

The Women's Voluntary Service used bicycles to deliver parcels to families distressed by the bombing and to keep in touch with one another.

The police were able to extend their beat patrols with bicycles.

Bicycles were often marked to show their use, as this machine for Air Raid Precaution.

Bicycles provided mobility to enable the police to warn of impending air raids.

The ARP needed bicycles for mobility. Many members used their own to respond quickly to an emergency.

the 1st and 6th Airborne Divisions which between them had thirteen parachute battalions and six battalions of Airlanding troops which would be deployed by glider. A typical battalion of parachute troops comprised of 600 men. The battalion was equipped with mortars, signals, machine guns and anti-tank weapons. The signals platoons contained a complement of eight bicycles.

With its experience in bicycle production, BSA was approached in 1941 with a request to develop a new item of equipment for the parachute troops. It was to be a bicycle but with specific parameters. It was to weigh no more than 22 pounds and be reliable for at least fifty miles travel on roads. It was explained to the designers that it was for use by airborne troops. The company produced a design with a folding frame and managed

This recreated Auxiliary Territorial Service girl depicting service with a mixed anti-aircraft battery showing how women in the armed forces used bicycles in their duties.

In the military bicycles were often marked to show what they were being used for.

to develop a machine which weighed 21 pounds. Road trials proved that it could meet distance criterion too. Wartime output of British military bicycles was around 120,000 machines, of which some 60,000 were produced by BSA.

The folding design concept went back over forty years. The Belgian army had used such a design in 1914 when riders collapsed their machines to carry them on their backs when crossing obstacles. In the British airborne battalions they were referred to as 'parabikes' and instead of being carried on his back, the parachutist would attach the bicycle to a rope during his descent so that it hit the ground just before he landed. There was also the option of dispatching the bicycle with its own parachute which would be recovered once on the ground. Glider-borne troops in the airlanding battalions could carry their bicycles collapsed to save space inside the aircraft. On landing the bicycles could be made ready to ride in around thirty seconds. These folding bicycles were deployed on D-Day and at

Other branches of the armed forces used bicycles, as demonstrated by this recreated RAF sergeant.

This recreated RAF pilot shows how bicycles were used to move around airfields.

During the Blitz on British cities many properties and businesses were destroyed, such as this building along with a stock of bicycles.

Arnhem. For Operation Varsity, the crossing of the Rhine on 24 March 1945, the British 1st Airborne Division loaded eighty bicycles into their Hamilcar gliders for use as liaison and delivering messages.

No other airborne unit appears to have used bicycles in a similar manner during the war. The Americans, who had at one time been so enthusiastic

British factory workers, in common with other countries, whether free or under German occupation, used bicycles as transport to get to work.

Civilians used whatever type of bicycle they could obtain, as shown by this selection.

As well as so-called 'parabikes' a small motorcycle called the 'Welbike' was developed for use by the airborne forces.

British airborne forces used gliders to deliver Jeeps to the battle area and these would carry bicycles for the troops.

about the military application of bicycles before the First World War, during which they did not use them, again considered the idea in the Second, once more abandoning them, this time in favour of motorcycles and later Jeeps which could be deployed from gliders and could be driven over rough terrain. These versatile 4x4 vehicles, which could carry l

oads of up to 800-pounds, several men, and tow a light anti-tank gun, were also used by the British airborne battalions. Jeeps were used to carry folding bicycles.

One exception to this was after the Japanese raid on Pearl Harbor. After the attack, America could not afford to be complacent and stepped up its state of readiness by increasing mounted patrols around the islands with troops, such as the 34th Infantry Regiment, using bicycles for the role.

When plans for the invasion of Britain were being drawn up in December 1939, consideration was given to equipping units of the *Fallschirmjäger* with bicycles. A design was produced for a folding machine, known as the *Fallschirmjäger Fahrrad*, and some were manufactured for field trials.

Of all the Allied forces to land on the beaches at Normandy only the Canadians and some British units waded ashore with bicycles. The machines were not always popular with the troops.

In the end, however, the German airborne units, like their American counterparts, did not recognise a role for bicycles. In that line of thinking they were joined by Italian and Japanese parachute troops who saw no use for the machines either. With the Russian airborne forces dismissing bicycles this left the British 1st and 6th Airborne Divisions in the unique position of being the only airborne formation to deploy and use service issue bicycles operationally during the war.

Chapter 13

The Wheels Move East:
Other Theatres of War

Between June 1940 and May 1943 the British army engaged the Italian army in North Africa. The fighting drew in German troops and eventually American troops. Conditions and terrain in the desert were harsh and not conducive to the use of bicycles meaning that, beyond very limited roles possibly in HQ rear areas far behind the main battle zones for liaison purposes, the machine played no part in the campaign.

On 22 June 1941 Hitler turned his armies eastwards towards Russia in Operation Barbarossa. In the fine weather of the summer months and relatively good road network the German army advanced deep into the country, overcoming all obstacles and pushing the Russian army back. All forms of transportation was used, including horse-drawn wagons, motor transport, and bicycles which could be ridden on the hard compact earthen roads in some parts of the country. By October the torrential rains turned these into impassable quagmires even worse than conditions on the Western Front in 1916 and 1917. Vehicles became bogged down, even tanks, and bicycles were abandoned. Then came the winter and the ground froze allowing vehicles to be driven for a time. However, the extreme cold of December 1941 reduced them to a frozen standstill. Here was another theatre of war where conditions and terrain made it impossible to use bicycles. Moreover, over the sheer distances involved of thousands of miles, bicycles were never going to be a feasible choice of transportation.

On 8 December, the Japanese 25th Army landed an amphibious force of 50,000 men at Kota Bharu on the northern end of the Malay Peninsula. At the time, the population of Japan was over 70 million from which some six million men would eventually be mobilised to serve in the armed forces. Many students volunteered to join military-style youth organizations. These recruits were given uniforms, armed with rifles and received training in tactics and handling weapons. That these young people were ready to serve their Emperor was perfect propaganda. It looked impressive, and being equipped with bicycles commentators could announce the students were independently mobile. Bicycles provided mass mobility in the most cost-effective manner. They were cheap, easy to produce and, best of all, they did not require fuel. Bicycle ownership in the country was between 8.6 and 10 million machines, an ownership ratio of about one to eight of the population.

The Japanese army had begun to introduce bicycles into service in the 1920s. In doing so they were copying what the British and Belgian armies had done in the First World War. Bicycle manufacturing in Japan had started as early as 1890 when the company of Miyata was founded. It was very successful, supplying bicycles to the army for the Russo-Japanese War in 1905 and also diversifying into rifle production. The company of Kuwahara Bicycles was established in 1918, producing machines for the local market and exporting to Russia in the 1920s. The company of Fuji was founded in 1899, produced bicycles for the Imperial Japanese Army which were used during the war. In the 1920s Japanese bicycle production formed a large part of the country's economy, with five million machines being produced in 1927 worth some 200 million Yen. In 1937 production had dropped to around one million bicycles per year with half being exported to China.

The bicycles used by Japanese troops tended to have solid frames and large wheels which could withstand the strain of carrying fully equipped soldiers, or pushed to transport equipment loads of up to eighty pounds. A small trailer with wheels was developed to be towed behind the bicycles so that bulky items could be transported. The bicycle allowed the Japanese soldier to carry far greater loads far more quickly.

In July 1941, as the eyes of the world were focussed on Hitler's runaway success in Russia, and with Holland and France under occupation by Germany, Japan, as Hitler's ally, seized the opportunity to occupy the Dutch East Indies and French Indo-China. For this a Japanese army of 140,000 was assembled which quickly spread out to establish control over the region, with troops entering the city of Saigon, either marching or riding on either bicycles or tanks. At the time Japan was not at war with either America or Britain. In seizing these territories, Japan now had access to oil, rubber, and other vital resources for its war effort.

Japan had meanwhile continued with its operations in China and bided its time while making plans before making its next move. When it did, things moved very fast. Admiral Isoroku Yamamoto, the architect of the attack against Pearl Harbor, had predicted that Japan would be able to 'run wild' for six months, after which time if America was not defeated the consequences would be disastrous. By 8/9 February 1942, forty days ahead of schedule, the first Japanese troops were crossing the Johor Strait separating mainland Malaya from Singapore. The Japanese had achieved this success with the help of bicycles which had been issued to the troops at the rate of 6,000 machines per division. One of these was the 5th Division which had advanced with tanks and other vehicles in support, but it was bicycles which provided the troops with their best and most adaptable means of mobility. When their rubber tyres wore out, the troops continued to ride on the metal wheel rims, making such a noise that the British and Commonwealth troops believed they were being attacked by tanks.

In general however, the Japanese did not neglect their bicycles. Two-man teams of mechanics were assigned to each company to repair and fix punctures. Troops sometimes rode for twenty hours a day and tyres became worn thin and shredded. The repair crews fixed dozens of punctures daily. Riders would follow pathways through the jungle which had been worn out by hunters and local natives, and sometimes they were able to appear behind the retreating Allies and catch them unawares. In the hands of the Japanese the bicycle was a 'go anywhere' form of transportation not requiring fuel. If a man did not have a bicycle and saw one in a village they were passing through he simply took it, that way Japanese troops ended up with many different types of bicycle.

When riders were faced with an obstacle, such as a river or ditch, they simply picked up their bicycles and carried them, or cut down trees to form an improvised bridge. Sometimes the troops walked, pushing their bicycles loaded with heavy equipment, or material for tasks such as bridge repair or building. Even senior officers took to riding bicycles during the campaign to scout ahead to assess damage to roads and bridges caused by the retreating Allies as they attempted to slow the

Japanese advance. Lieutenant Colonel Yosuke Yokoyama, commanding the 15th Engineer Regiment attached to the 5th Infantry Division, was one such officer, riding ahead to direct the damage repair. He would later do the same on New Guinea. The Japanese cyclists were known as the 'Peddling army' and some historians consider the bicycle to have been Japan's secret weapon in the Malay campaign. It is a debatable point, but bicycles certainly helped.

During their month-long advance the Japanese captured great quantities of stores which they loaded onto their bicycles, which they pushed as improvised wheelbarrows. Colonel Tsuji Masanobu, Chief of Operations and Planning Staff of the 25th Army, wrote: 'the excellent paved roads, and the cheap Japanese bicycles, the assault on Malaya was easy… even the long-legged Englishmen could not escape our troops on bicycles.'

When they went into action, bicycle riders would dismount and leave their bicycles behind in a central location with a handful of troops to guard them. After the action and the advance resumed, to save time the troops looking after the bicycles would induce locals to push the machines forward instead of the surviving troops returning to retrieve their bicycles. The Japanese did not have it all their own way, and there were cases of Australian troops managing to turn the tables and isolate the cycle troops from their accompanying motorized forces. By destroying a bridge, say, over a river, the motorised vehicles were brought to a halt. The cycle troops would pick up their machines and moved forward as infantry, and the Allied troops could take advantage of the weakened force.

No great skill was required to learn how to ride a bicycle. If one has good balance the main hurdle, how to stay upright, has been mastered. The other elements, such as how to steer and manoeuvre will naturally fall into place. To the Japanese soldier, having a bicycle was a privilege and owning one was regarded as a valuable resource. When men were sent to other garrisons, such as the captured islands of Tarawa, Iwo Jima and Saipan, they took their prized bicycles with them. There are accounts from later in the war when the Americans landed to recapture these islands they were bemused to see bicycles strewn around amidst the other debris of battle.

By 15 February 1942, Singapore was in Japanese hands. Twelve hundred miles to the north, at the other end of the Malay Peninsula, Japanese troops captured Rangoon. On 8 December 1941 Japanese troops had begun to land on the island of Luzon in the Philippines. By 22 December they had 43,000 men on the island. Some used bicycles during the campaign to speed up their advance against the American defenders and local Filipino troops. In one incident, a group of around 300 Japanese cyclists were approaching Manila when they were fired on by American and Filipino troops causing them to dismount and scatter. They suffered heavy casualties. The incident proved how vulnerable bicycle troops were when advancing, something which had been identified early on when the bicycle was being considered as transportation for infantry. On 2 January 1942, photo-journalist Carl Mydans, working for *Life* magazine, observed from his hotel window how Japanese troops 'came up the boulevards…riding on bicycles and on tiny motorcycles.' The force of 151,000 American and Filipino troops managed to hold out for fifteen weeks until lack of resources forced them to surrender on 9 June 1942.

When the British army engaged the Japanese in Burma and along the Malay Peninsula, the conditions of deep jungle prevented the use of bicycles.

Elsewhere the Japanese continued to expand their military sphere to seize the Dutch East Indies of Java and Sumatra with their rubber plantations. This allowed them to manufacture tyres for the army's vehicles and bicycles while denying the resource to the Allies. This loss of rubber was a problem to the Allies.

The Pacific islands, such as Saipan, Tarawa, Iwo Jima and Okinawa, varied greatly in terrain: one would have swamps, another would have black volcanic sand. Guadalcanal was attacked on 7 August 1942 where fighting lasted until 9 February 1943. The conditions there were described by a veteran of the campaign: 'a rough, volcanic island. The streams that lead down to the sea are filled with heavy jungle but the ridges in between were covered with tall grass that grew to a height of eight to ten feet. In the earlier fighting of the Marines and the American Division this grass was burned off, leaving the ridges bare, but the stream valleys still filled with jungle. We surrounded the Japanese in the valleys by seizing the ridges. It was tough fighting because the ridges were quite narrow.'

In such conditions the use of troops on bicycles could never be considered an option.

The Americans encountered fierce resistance on Saipan, on which the US Marines landed on 15 June 1944. Two days later the 23rd Marines were advancing towards Fina Susu Ridge, where Japanese were known to be in defensive positions. As they moved forward some marines noticed the unusual sight of a lone Japanese soldier riding a bicycle, from which they concluded he must be a messenger carrying orders between positions. Bicycles for military use were almost unknown in the Pacific island campaign. Bicycles will only be useful where conditions are appropriate.

The Japanese army used bicycles throughout the war in its campaigns in China and Malaya and the war on the islands across the Pacific.

It is estimated that by the end of the war the Japanese army lost three million bicycles.

Chapter 14

Second Front:
The Allies Return to Europe

In the four years during which the German army held France and the rest of Europe under occupation, standards of living conditions gradually deteriorated. One reason for this was that the transportation system could not cope. Railway workers would not cooperate and even risked their lives by going on strike. In Holland, the Dutch Resistance organised strikes on the railways in 1941 and again in 1943. Such action was not without its dangers and many workers who did not cooperate were either shot or deported. In June 1943 the British and Americans came up with Operation Pointblank to disrupt the transportation system supplying the German army. The RAF bombed at night and the USAAF bombed by day, allowing the defenders no respite. In February 1944, the success of Pointblank led to a new aerial offensive codenamed the Transport Plan, which was intended to destroy the German rail network and sever oil supplies. Between March 1944 and March 1945 the bombing reduced German petrol stocks from 134,000 to 39,000 tons and diesel from 100,000 to 39,000 tons. This meant severe rationing and more troops were forced to use bicycles, either service machines or those taken from civilians.

In 1942 a series of operations against targets along the coast of German-occupied France kept Hitler guessing when the Allies might invade occupied Europe. On 19 August 1942, British and Canadian troops, together with a contingent of fifty US Rangers, landed in the port of Dieppe. All the tanks were lost and of the 10,500 engaged 1,500 Canadians were killed or wounded and 2,000 taken prisoner. The Germans brought in troops to contain the attack, including infantry riding bicycles from the garrison at Le Petit-Appeville.

Not all of the operations were so unsuccessful, but the Allies learned valuable lessons from each. The planning for the liberation of Europe also involved sending SOE agents into France, Holland and Belgium, 600 male and 50 female, to gather information concerning German plans and defences. They supported and were supported by local resistance groups. Allied agents found bicycles to be essential for transport.

Operation Husky, the invasion of Sicily, was a combined amphibious and airborne assault launched on 9 July 1943. The campaign on the island lasted a hard-fought six weeks which ended with many Italians and Germans surrendering, but more escaped across the waterway of the Messina Strait to reach mainland Italy. The Allies followed seventeen days later to cross into Italy on 3 September. Ahead of them lay a hard campaign which would last until the end of the war in May 1945. Bicycles were used to a limited degree during the campaign on Sicily where the Canadian 1st Battalion Hastings and Prince Edward Regiment, part of the 1st Brigade of the 1st Canadian Division, probably used them to conduct local liaison duties and to deliver messages and orders. Some bicycles were used by airborne forces for the same purpose. Overall, however, the terrain and conditions, coupled with the type of fighting, on Sicily and later in Italy, meant that bicycles were not usable. Resistance groups on the Italian mainland, known as *gappisti*, patriotic action groups or partisans, used bicycles in actions against the Germans, which increased in intensity after Italy's capitulation in 1943.

The first American troops began to arrive in Britain in 1942 with numbers increasing throughout 1943 as the build-up for the invasion of Europe grew apace. Everything was brought over, with hundreds of thousands of every size of vehicle from small, powerful Jeeps to heavyweight recovery vehicles and tanks. Nothing was left to chance and nothing was overlooked as fuel, food and other supplies arrived in unimaginable tonnages in preparation to support the combined operation.

The German army had been in occupation of Europe for four years, during which time it had been busy consolidating its newly-won conquests and turning the Continent into a fortress. Thousands of bunkers containing heavy guns had been built, along with other positions containing machine guns and mortars all overlapping firepower and protected by belts of minefields and barbed wire. This was Hitler's formidable 'Atlantic Wall' stretching over 1,600 miles from Norway to the border with Spain. The forces of occupation held down more than 1.5 million troops, of which

As the build-up for D-Day increased hundreds of thousands of vehicles arrived and some bicycles were also sent over.

Troops would often use bicycles as a quick and easy way to get around.

over 600,000 would be committed to the coming battle in France. One of the units defending the Normandy coastline was the LXXXIV Corps, commanded by General Eric Marcks, which was responsible for a stretch of some 250 miles, included the Channel Islands. The Corps had three lines of troops, with the front line comprising three divisions, including the 716 and 709 Infantry Divisions, each of which had built up good local knowledge of the area where they expected to fight, but most troops in the battalions had either little or no combat experience. The second reserve line included the 30th Infantry Brigade and the 352nd and 243rd Infantry Divisions. The 352nd and 243rd benefitted from having just been reorganised and had more experienced and better trained troops, some of which were formed into *Fahrradbewegliches* or bicycle infantry battalions. The 30th Brigade also included battalions of bicycle infantry with around 1,200 men. The third line had two more divisions which were considered as reinforcements.

In April 1944, the 6th Fallschirmjäger Regiment with three battalions had been added to the units defending the Atlantic Wall. Each battalion had a mortar company and an anti-tank company along with an engineer platoon and a bicycle reconnaissance platoon. By June, on the eve of the Allied landings, the engineer and bicycle platoons had been increased to company strength and additional weapons companies had been added to the regimental structure which now included anti-aircraft defence.

Some of the bicycle battalions which now found themselves in what would be the front line when the Allies attacked had been formed as recently as the beginning of 1944. For example, the restructuring of the 921st and 922nd Grenadier Regiments of the 243rd Infantry Division began their restructuring with bicycles in January that year, while the 920th Grenadier Regiment relied almost entirely on horses for transportation.

Only five days before the Allies' attack, the two Panzergrenadier regiments of 17 SS-Panzergrenadier Division Götz von Berlichingen had a motorised vehicle allocation of more than 1,700 trucks, but shortage of fuel meant that they were forced to resort to bicycles for transportation. The Germans piled the bicycles with weapons such as anti-tank Panzerfausts and heavy loads of ammunition. They were so heavily laden that they often had to be pushed by hand. In the later stages of the fighting in eastern France in September 1944, specialist groups of infantry were

By 1944 the German army was facing a fuel crisis and using bicycles was a simple solution to moving troops quickly, as shown in this image using re-enactors.

The re-enactors demonstrate how the Germans used a combination of armour, artillery and troops either in truck or on bicycles to fight back the Allies.

Even units of the much-vaunted SS had to resort to bicycles, as shown in this recreated image.

formed into anti-tank teams, armed with Panzerschreck or Panzerfaust rocket-launchers, which continued to use bicycles.

In March 1944 two of the six battalions of infantry forming part of the 17th SS Panzergrenadier Division were using bicycles, because, not requiring fuel or fodder, they were more economical.

At the start of the war the German army had benefitted from excellent radio communications at all levels, including ground to air. However by 1944, with reverses and enormous losses on all fronts, this advantage had been lost. Output of radio equipment could not replace these losses. Nowhere was this felt more than in France, where headquarters companies of infantry battalions had to resort back to the old-fashioned method of using runners on bicycles to deliver messages. This was far from ideal, but better than nothing.

In the months leading up to the invasion the RAF and USAAF had been engaged in another bombing campaign to destroy road and rail networks in the Normandy area, to prevent supplies reaching the front. When the battle started, Allied aircraft dominated the skies over the Normandy beachheads and they could engage any column of vehicles not identified with the Allied white star symbol. Troops soon found out it was safer and faster to move on bicycles. Small numbers of bicycles were not so obvious when moving on roads and they could be screened from overhead by trees. As the Normandy campaign widened, the use of bicycles by the German army in France increased and troops often seized machines from the local populace. After four years of occupation many of these were without tyres which had been substituted by binding rope around the wheels. In Holland the people used wooden tyres to replace rubber. To the three million standard service issue bicycles used by the German army in the war must be added the millions of civilian machines commandeered from the people in the occupied countries.

The Normandy landings would be supported by three airborne divisions landed with the order to secure strategic points to allow movement inland. To the east the British 6th Airborne Division would land, where elements would seize the bridges at Bénouville, spanning the Caen Canal and Orne River, neutralise a heavy gun battery at Merville and destroy bridges over the Troan River. Probably the most important of these targets were the bridges at Bénouville, because the Germans could use them to send troops to attack the British beaches. For the British, it was important they be captured because they would be able to move east to expand their position.

On the night of 5/6 June 1944, parachute landings were made in advance of the beach assault to secure the positions. At the eastern end, the bridges at Bénouville were seized intact just after midnight by glider-borne troops of the Oxfordshire & Buckinghamshire Light Infantry in the Air Landing Brigade of 6th Airborne Division. The commanding officer, Major John Howard, had been given orders he was to hold his position until relieved. As dawn approached Howard's position was struggling to hold off German attacks. He had received some support by men of 7th Battalion Parachute Regiment who began to arrive around 3 pm to replace the losses to his original ninety men. His position was far from being secure but he was determined to hold the bridges as ordered.

On Sword Beach, the most easterly landing beach, the first of 29,000 troops of British 3rd Infantry Division was due to begin coming ashore at 7.25 am. The first brigade to land was the 8th commanded by Brigadier Cass. Attached to 8th Brigade was the 1st Special Service Brigade, commanded by Lord Lovat who had taken part in various Commando operations, including the ill-fated Dieppe raid in 1942. The 1st SSB comprised No 3 Commando, No 4 Commando and No 6 Commando along with 45 Royal Marine Commando which would begin to land around 8.40 am. No 6 Commando, commanded by Lieutenant Colonel Derek Mills-Roberts, was tasked with a special mission, for which it was issued with bicycles. They had been ordered to move inland rapidly and head east towards Bénouville, a distance of about six miles, where they would link up with and reinforce Major Howard's D Company of the 2nd Ox & Bucks Light Infantry who were still holding the bridges. It was imperative they be reached because the bridges had to be held.

As No 6 Commando landed around the area of La Brèche the men were urged forward to clear the beach by their officers, such as Major Pat Porteous who had won the Victoria Cross in the Dieppe operation. One of the men following the directions was Corporal Peter Masters, on secondment to No 6 Commando from No 10 Commando to act as an interpreter, now attached to No 3 (Cycle) Troop, commanded by Captain 'Robbo' Robinson. The forty-four men in the troop mounted their bicycles and headed south in the direction of Colleville-sur-Mer, which put them behind the German coastal defences. Here they could turn east and follow the road towards Bénouville.

As they approached the town, the troops had been cycling through enemy held territory for three hours when they had their first contact with German troops who fired on them from houses on the outskirts of the town. The troop sustained a few casualties which caused them to dismount and take cover. Captain Robinson turned to Corporal Masters, saying, 'Now there's something you can do.' Robinson ordered Masters to go forward by himself to assess the situation. As he tentatively advanced he was fired on. His weapon jammed and could not return fire, so Masters resorted to shouting at the Germans to surrender. A brief firefight erupted and the Germans vacated the buildings to take up new positions in another building from where they continued to fire. Captain Robinson ordered his troop to charge with fixed bayonets, forcing the Germans out of the house. The appearance of a British tank which fired on the German positions cleared the way for Robinson, who resumed his journey by bicycle towards the Bénouville bridges which he reached around 1 pm. By now Major Howard had been holding the bridges for over thirteen hours and, as more reinforcements continued to arrive, including Lord Lovat, the position at the bridges became increasingly secure. Bicycles played a crucial role in this action.

Over to the west, the American 82nd and 101st Airborne Divisions would land to secure the town of Ste Mere Église and the roads leading off the beach at Utah. One of those men taking part in the action was Private Ken Russell of F Company, 505th PIR, whose unit engaged a group of German soldiers moving through the town on bicycles.

As the Allied landings developed strength and the troops began to move further inland, the Germans had to react to a constant stream of reports which put Allied troops seemingly everywhere. One of those reports, at around 12.15 pm, had been about troops mounted on bicycles advancing towards the town of St Aubin d'Arquenay from the direction of Ouistreham, which were the leading troops of Lord Lovat's Special Service Brigade.

Another unit to land on Sword Beach was the 2nd Battalion King's Shropshire Light Infantry (KSLI), part of 185th Brigade coming in with the second wave. By 11 am the battalion had advanced as far as Hermanville, but on discovering their tank support from the Staffordshire Yeomanry of 27th Armoured Brigade had not arrived, the commanding officer, Lieutenant Colonel F.J. Maurice, grabbed a bicycle and pedalled back to the beach to find out why the tanks were not where they should have been. The problem was not enemy action, but a massive traffic jam caused on the beach slowing everything down to a grinding pace. Having discovered the root of the problem, Maurice rode back to Hermanville where he reported to his brigade commander, Brigadier Smith, who ordered the brigade to continue its advance on Caen without waiting for the tanks to catch up. In this instance, the bicycle had proved to be the fastest means of transportation in the chaos of vehicles edging forward from the beachhead. Bicycles were keeping senior officers mobile and maintaining lines of communications.

On other beaches, bicycles were also proving of value. At the coastal village of Bernières on the Canadian beach of Juno, where 21,500 troops would land, the traffic from 9th Brigade caused heavy congestion and eventually it was only the cyclist troops, such as the Highland Light Infantry of Canada, or infantry on foot, which could move freely through the chaos. Further inland, civilians were riding their bicycles around the city of Caen, announcing to all they saw that the Allies had landed. Not that they needed to be told because the noise of the battle told the news for itself, but that did not stop them. During the planning stage of the operation, Montgomery had expected Caen to be taken on D-Day itself. It would be more than another month before it was finally captured.

Not all the troops who landed found the bicycles to be as useful as Colonel Maurice. To the west, on Gold Beach, the 2nd Battalion South Wales Borderers landed as part of 56th Brigade, the independent reinforcement brigade, with 50th Northumbrian Division. As he was leaving his landing craft, Private W.H. Edwards was told to grab a bicycle and take it with him as he went ashore. Looking at the water he was about to enter, and not knowing its depth, Edwards told his officer he could not swim. With no time to waste arguing trivialities, Edwards was accused of holding up the invasion and relieved of the bicycle. Being deprived of it might have saved his life, because as he left the landing craft he was immediately knocked over by a wave. Still loaded with his personal equipment he was in danger of being dragged underwater and only rescued from drowning by a passing soldier who pulled him out.

The 9th Battalion Durham Light Infantry, forming part of the 151st Brigade of the 50th (Northumbrian) Division, was another unit of the 25,000 men landing on Gold Beach. Charles Eagles was one of the men coming ashore: 'There were sighs of relief all round. I think it was at this point that we were told to grab some folding paratroop bikes. I tell you, after everything else, that's all we needed. I must confess, I couldn't see me with my original backpack, a rifle and a bike… What a comical sight to any German observer… The order to mount was duly given, truly a sight for sore eyes as we wobbled all over … some of us had not ridden a bike for years. After two or three hundred yards, all hell broke loose as some shellfire flew around us… We were showered with debris, and all ended up in the ditches… Nobody got on their bikes again, we just sort of forgot to take them with us; it was quite funny really, and I can't recall any NCO, or officer for that matter, mentioning the word "bike" ever again.'

The Germans may have considered the sight of British troops on bicycles 'funny' but they would also have regarded the method of transportation as sensible. They had been forced to use bicycles due to fuel shortages, and now here they were using bicycles for operational purposes to counter the landings. According to Oberst Fritz Ziegelman, Chief of Staff with 352nd Division, at least three battalions of the 915 Regiment were deployed on bicycles to patrol the unit's operational area east of Bayeux and between Villers to the north and St Leger to the south. At around 4 am that morning, Lieutenant General Dietrich Kraiss, commanding the 352nd Division, responsible for defending the coastline along the Gold Beach sector, where Private Eagles would land, extending westwards into the Omaha Beach sector, where the American 1st and 29th Infantry Divisions would land, ordered a battalion mounted on bicycles to go in search of reported landings of parachute troops. In the event, the reports turned out to be false and the parachute troops, known as 'Ruperts' to confuse the Germans, were decoys.

Three weeks after the initial landings the Allies had landed more than 875,000 men. During that time the Germans had lost over 29,000 men and received only 6,000 replacements. Over the coming weeks, as the fighting moved further inland, reinforcement troops were still landing with bicycles. Another to find his bicycle an encumbrance was Lieutenant David Priest of the 5th Battalion Duke of Cornwall's Light Infantry who landed at Gold Beach on 24 June as part of 214th Brigade of the 43rd Wessex Division. Designated as bicycle troops, Priest remembered training to ride a bicycle while wearing full kit, and how 'the thing' was inclined to 'rear up on you'. Much to their relief, the battalion was ordered to park their bicycles, never to be seen again. But these abandoned bicycles would have been used by other troops, probably serving in the rear echelon areas engaged in logistical tasks, or by messengers. Some would have been used by the troops to pay visits on newly-liberated French civilians. Locals too would not have missed the opportunity claim discarded military bicycles to replace the ones taken from them during the four years of German occupation.

Over the coming weeks the Allies would progress towards Paris. The German commandant of Paris, General von Choltitz, claimed that he was supposed to have 25,000 men to hold the city, but in fact had just a few aged soldiers, four tanks, an assortment of old captured French vehicles, an anti-aircraft unit and some companies of infantry on bicycles.

As the Germans retreated they used bicycles from any source that came to hand, especially civilians.

This recreated image shows how the Germans often loaded heavy amounts of equipment onto their bicycles.

The manoeuvres by the Allies had had the effect of enveloping the Germans and forcing them into a wholesale retreat eastwards along a corridor known as the 'Falaise Gap' through which the remnants of the German army escaped between 12 and 21 August. Onlookers saw whole columns of retreating Germans moving along the Argentan–Falaise road where: 'the floor of the valley was seen to be alive with stuff. Men marching, cycling and running, columns of horse-drawn transport and motor transport.' Much materiel was abandoned, but bicycles were a valuable asset and greatly prized as transportation. During the retreat twenty men from a bicycle company from the Fallschirmjäger Regiment 6, a parachute regiment fighting as infantry, showed how the Germans were still far from being beaten. The bicycle company together with a single surviving Mk IV tank from the notorious 2nd SS Das Reich Division turned their weight on a battalion of American infantry and captured 13 officers and 600 other ranks.

The Allies were now on the move. Speed and mobility were crucial factors at this stage in the war. On 25 August Paris was liberated. On

2 September, General Brian Horrocks, commanding British XXX Corps, had gathered officers of the Guards Armoured Division at his HQ in Douai and briefed them to advance on Brussels with all haste. The Guards' Sherman tanks and other armoured vehicles covered the eighty miles to enter and liberate the city the following day. Some units along the 700-mile-wide front were advancing twenty miles a day or more. The speed of the advance ruled out troops riding bicycles, although motor vehicles sometimes carried bicycles in case they were needed. In the First World War it was the static lines and the mud which prevented the use of bicycles; now in 1944 it was the speed of the advance. The Germans retreated in cars or trucks if they had them, until the fuel ran out. For the rest, they either walked or rode bicycles, many of which had been taken from civilians.

On 5 September, rumours began to circulate in Holland that the town of Breda, five miles from the Dutch border had been liberated, leading to a spontaneous outbreak of celebrations. For a young girl called Annick van Hardeveld, a nurse in Amsterdam and member of a resistance group, the news proved fatal. Reacting to the rumour, she was riding her bicycle

The Germans took bicycles from any source and demanded a fixed quota be handed over in countries under occupation.

to meet fellow resistance fighters, wearing a Dutch flag draped over her nurse's uniform, no doubt in anticipation of impending liberation. A member of the much-hated and feared *Ordnungspolizei* saw her from his car and shot her dead.

The Allies had liberated Antwerp the day before and the Dutch were now eagerly anticipating their turn. The Germans were retreating so fast (and stealing so many bicycles) the period was referred to as 'Dolle Dinsdag' (Mad Tuesday). During the occupation the Germans had stripped Holland of 60,000 privately owned vehicles, 4,000 buses, and two million bicycles. For many years after the war the Dutch could taunt Germans with 'Geef me min fieti' (give me my bike). One of the retreating troops to make use of an acquired bicycle was Sergeant Erich Hensel serving with a signals company. He had been wounded in the leg and later remembered the constant delays during the retreat. Another with memories of that retreat was Lieutenant Heinz Volz, serving as adjutant in the 1st Battalion Fallschirmjäger Regiment von Hofmann. He knew that order had to be restored if they were to hold off the Allies. On 10 September at Udenhout he remembered how this was partially achieved: 'everything possible [had been done] in the three available days to equip ourselves appropriately for the coming operations. Above all we tried to get at least most of the soldiers equipped with bicycles to make the unit more mobile.'

Holland had to wait another eight months before it was finally liberated on 5 May 1945. The German army had not given up the war just yet and showed the Allies just how much fight it had left by defeating the British 1st Airborne Division in Operation Market Garden. The plan had been conceived by General Montgomery with the intention of using the American 82nd and 101st Airborne Divisions to seize bridges across the waterways at Eindhoven, Grave, Son, and Nijmegen, with the British 1st Airborne Division to capture the bridge at Arnhem to cross the Rhine into Germany. The American airborne elements went well, but for the British at Arnhem things went disastrously wrong.

Unusually for American units, some used bicycles: the 2/327th Glider Infantry Regiment attached to the 101st Airborne Division, the HQ Company, which landed east of the Son Bridge and being glider-landed could carry the extra load; and the 326th Airborne Engineer Battalion attached to the 101st Airborne Division. Private First Class Oscar Mendoza of B Company from the battalion demonstrated great initiative when he acquired a tricycle-style machine to deliver supplies which had been scattered during air-drops. Mendoza had landed in the vicinity of Eerde where he was wounded. After treatment he refused to be evacuated and used the unofficial service tricycle, with its large capacity front-mounted cargo, to support his fellow airborne troops.

In response to the first landings on 17 September, the Germans deployed quickly, especially to the British landings around Arnhem, where troops began to form up. Some troops arrived by motor vehicle, some rode horses; bicycles were a simple option, as observed by Staff-Sergeant Erwin Heck, who saw them arriving faster than men on foot. Even the elite SS resorted to bicycles, such as Panzer-Grenadier Regiment 21 of the 10th SS 'Frundsberg' Division which used them to cover the thirty-mile distance from Deventer to Arnhem.

Another unit to use bicycles was 'Kampfgruppe von Tettau', named after Generalleutnant Hans von Tettau, who was in charge of military training in the Dutch Command at Arnhem. It was a composite unit which included three battalions from the SS NCO Training School at Arnhem, at least nine vintage tanks of French origin and other infantry units, including SS Battalion Eberwein. Tettau deployed against the western fringe around the landing zone on Ginkel Heath. On 21 September he was joined by 700 men from the Worrowski Battalion, who had ridden their bicycles, each man with his complete kit, seventy-five miles from Katwijk an Zee, just north of Rotterdam. Lance Corporal 'Ginger' Wilson of the 1st Battalion Border Regiment saw the approach and recalled there 'seemed to be hundreds of Germans like a football crowd'. One to arrive with this unit was Herbert Kessler, a 19-year old NCO serving with the Herman Goering Training Regiment. He recalled: 'Rumour had it that we were earmarked to become a reserve for countering further parachute landings.' They had been on the move since receiving their orders on 19 September. As they approached the area of Ginkel Heath the column came under fire, which Kessler remembered as 'a strafing run by low-flying aircraft, the order came to clear a patch of woods where it was suspected enemy paratrooper stragglers were located. Nothing was found except for the dead of the first few days of fighting; clear evidence of the grim events that had taken place.' Over the next couple of days the Worrowski Battalion were involved in heavy fighting around the area.

Being cyclists the battalion was independently mobile, could react faster than troops on foot, and could use smaller roads and lanes inaccessible to larger motorised vehicles. They were joined by some members of the *Reichsarbeitsdienst* – the labour corps which used many bicycles – and together were ordered to head south past the Hotel Wolfheze heading towards Heveadorp using these smaller roads. Kessler remembers how the battalion 'turned off the road to the right onto a forest trail, where they halted, packed closely together. So far they could see there was no trace of the enemy. But this was to change soon. The soldiers were sitting on their bicycles without a care in the world when they were surprised by a murderous machine gun fire from the flank.' Kessler and his comrades had relaxed their vigilance and been caught unawares by an unseen British observation post established in a tower by the Westerbouwing Inn where the 1st Battalion Border Regiment had sited a machine gun. After the initial shock, the group gathered itself and launched a counter-attack. Over the coming days the remnants of the Worrowski Battalion fought on foot as dismounted infantry having stored their bicycles. During the period of fighting von Tettau's unit lost heavily, including tanks destroyed by PIATs. For nine days the British troops defended the bridge at Arnhem in the vain hope XXX Corps would arrive. The operation ended on 25 September and out of the 10,000 British troops used in the operation, 8,000 were killed, wounded or taken prisoner.

Three months later, on 28 December, Hitler ordered what would be his last offensive directed against the Allies in the West. This was Operation Nordwind which would become better known as 'The Battle of the Bulge'. In these battles bicycles were not used by either side. The scope and scale, along with conditions in weather and terrain, prevented their use. However, for the German army the wartime role of the bicycle was far from over, as would be shown during the fighting in Berlin as the Russians closed in from the east.

Chapter 15

The Battle for Berlin

By mid-April 1945 Berlin had been encircled by the Russians. Defences around the city collapsed in the face of Russian attacks. One experienced soldier to find himself in Berlin at the time was Corporal Helmut Fromm, who was in the Konev sector trying to hold the position on the Seelow Heights. He recalled: 'We had to pull back. I was left with a machine gun and two men. I'm the only one who knows how to use a [Panzer] Faust – most of the others have only done office work. Then we rode very fast on bicycles up the Breslau-Berlin autobahn.' All the while he was being fired on.

In October 1944 Hitler ordered the creation of the Volkssturm (Peoples' Guard), intended to provide manpower for the forthcoming defence of

This recreated image shows how the Volkssturm was made up of men of all ages and used bicycles with Panzerfaust to help defend Berlin.

Germany using men aged between 16 to 60 who were not already serving in the military. The Volkssturmmänner included veterans of the First War and even amputees from the Second.

Uniforms were in short supply and members of the Volkssturm wore their own clothes that they might have worn for going to work. The only official item of uniform was an armband with the title 'Deutscher Volkssturm Wehrmacht'. They used various captured and obsolete weapons, some left over from the Great War. The more fortunate units were equipped with K98 service rifles and even Panzerfaust to slow down the advancing Soviet T-34 tanks. The intention was to raise a force of six million men.

Despite the backing of Goebbels and Himmler, membership never reached the levels Hitler imagined. On 19 April 1945 when the Russians broke through from the Seelow Heights to the east of Berlin there were perhaps 100 battalions of Volkssturm in the city, moving from one location to another either on foot or bicycles, which by now were becoming scarce. In battle the Volkssturm came under the command of the army, but their

By 1945 the Germans were fighting in the defence of Berlin using short-range anti-tank weapons called Panzerfaust which could be carried on bicycles.

This recreated scene shows how German troops rode bicycles into battle in Berlin armed with Panzerfaust.

fighting ability was doubtful and many ran away. Those who stood and fought were armed with Panzerfaust or Panzerschreck. The defending Germans at this stage had more bicycles than tanks and trucks combined.

Another formation raised in 1944 was the Volksgrenadier Division, composed of two types of infantry regiments. The first being the infantry battalion which included 100 bicycles; the second being the Grenadier Regiment auf Fahrradern, equipped with 700 bicycles for around 1,800 men.

It was possible to carry several Panzerfaust, weighing 15 pounds and measuring 32 inches, on a bicycle. Groups of three or four men could operate together to form a tank-hunting group to ambush vehicles. The Panzerschreck, another shoulder-fired weapon, was bigger at five feet long. The projectile weighed 7.25 pounds. The Panzerfaust was disposable, the Panzerschreck could be reloaded. A man on a bicycle could just about manage to keep control while carrying a launcher tube with several projectiles in containers attached to his bicycle. These cyclist anti-tank

Some troops could attach several Panzerfaust to their bicycles which were useful to get around the devastated city.

troops would dismount, stack their bicycles, and take up position behind cover in readiness to engage a target, either an approaching vehicle or a target of opportunity. To engage a tank at such close quarters, because of the limited range of the weapons, took nerve. Over the coming weeks, as the Russians continued to advance on Berlin, there would be plenty of opportunities to put this tactic into practice.

On 24 April the forces of the two senior Russian commanders, Generals Koniev and Zhukov, linked up south-west of the city. Amid the chaos, boys of the Volkssturm, the Hitler Youth, even members of the RAD, ran between destroyed buildings to take up defensive positions, or carried messages on foot or riding bicycles. For more than a week the fighting continued from one building to the next. Finally, on 2 May the last of the German defenders surrendered to the Russians and the fighting came to a standstill. Over the days that followed, leading up to the official German signing of the document of surrender on 7 May, the few remaining serviceable bicycles left in the city became a valuable commodity. People were desperate to leave Berlin to escape the Russians. For many of the Russian soldiers, especially those coming from more remote regions, this was the first time they had ever seen a bicycle. Bicycles became the main method of transportation for the German refugees heading west towards the British and American lines to escape the alternative of being under rule by Communist Russia.

Chapter 16

Wheels in the Cold War

After 1945 bicycles had been in service with some armies for over sixty years, having been used in two global wars and numerous small-scale conflicts. When bicycles were first used, tanks had not even been invented. The armies of the industrially powerful nations were motorised and bicycles were an anachronism from days gone by. Few countries kept bicycles in their standing armies, exceptions being Sweden and Finland, which held on to them for special duties.

But while they were not used by standing armies, they were still used in some conflicts. When the Malayan Emergency started in June 1948, Britain sent troops to quell the unrest and protect British interests. Over the next twelve years of war, many bicycles would be used. The Malayan National Liberation Army, lacking the technology to support motorised transport in the jungle, used bicycles to transport supplies. Bicycles made perfect sense to these rebel forces. They were simple to handle, needed no fuel and only basic maintenance, and were quiet and easily concealed. All of these points, and the fact they could blend in with normal daily life, made them one of the most effective pieces of equipment available to such forces.

France was faced with trouble in its overseas colony of French Indo-China from 1945 when the army became engaged in a war against the tenacious Communist-backed regime of the Vietminh. The rebels and other insurgent forces were usually client states of Russia or China fighting to achieve national independence, political recognition or some other aim. The French army suffered a humiliating defeat at Dien Bien Phu when the garrison of 15,000 men at the heavily fortified base became surrounded by over 50,000 Vietminh troops of Ho Chi Minh and Nguyen Vo. For 56 days between 13 March and 7 May, the French tried to keep the garrison supplied with air drops and parachuting in reinforcements. The Vietminh army was supplied by a column of some 60,000 men and women pushing bicycles laden with food, ammunition and other supplies. The bicycles were fitted with extemporised modifications such as lengths of bamboo attached to the handlebars for control as they pushed the machines, which they called 'xe tho' (pack bikes) or 'ngua thep' (steel horses). Each was capable of transporting loads of 400 pounds. Ironically, the bicycles used by the Vietminh were French-built by Peugeot. They enabled the transportation of an estimated 2,000 tons of supplies in the siege. For all the sophistication the French deployed during the war, which included helicopters, it was the low-tech, basic 'man with a bicycle' which endured and won through. The Vietminh would return to the bicycle again in another war against a much larger enemy.

During the Korean War of 1950 to 1953 a coalition of allied countries from the United Nations, including Britain, America, Australia, Greece, France, Holland and Canada, faced the army of North Korea, which was supported by the Communist regime of China and, to a lesser degree, Soviet Russia. The United Nations relied on motor vehicles and air power to provide support and transportation. The Communist forces used a range of military hardware supplied by China and Russia, along with stocks of captured Japanese weapons and supplies from the Second World War. At one point the Chinese leader, Mao Tse Tung, approached Stalin to supply his army with 3,500 trucks and 2,000 bicycles.

Between 1955 and 1975 America would bring to bear all the technological resources at its disposal in an effort to defeat the Communist forces of North Vietnam. It would see air power deployed on an unprecedented scale and include widespread use of helicopters to transport troops to operational zones. The Communist forces were known as 'Vietcong' but were essentially the same as those who had forced out the French several years earlier. The Vietcong had very little in the way of technology in response to America's overwhelming weaponry, and to compensate for this it turned to China and Soviet Russia to assist it. In the 1950s Russia had supplied the North Vietnamese with 600 trucks and 64,000 bicycles. Against the USA, China was to prove the staunchest supplier of equipment to North Vietnam. The one thing which the country had in abundance was manpower which would achieve incredible feats of engineering to build roads through jungles. The work was also undertaken by women who were as committed to the war as any man in Ho Chi Minh's army.

The first bicycles to be seen in China were ridden by Europeans and viewed as a curiosity, but the idea caught on. Bicycle manufacturing was established in China in the 1890s and they soon became popular. Workers used them. Even prostitutes, known as 'sing-song' girls, used them when

Porters pushing bicycles laden with supplies through the jungle helped the Vietcong win the war in Vietnam.

In the 1960s during America's involvement in Vietnam, the Vietcong used thousands of bicycles to move vast amounts of supplies along the Ho Chi Minh Trail.

they frequented the waterfront to visit international sailors in Shanghai harbour. By 1958 Chinese factories were producing a million bicycles a year and it was never a problem supplying them to Vietnam in its wars against France and America. North Vietnam produced bicycles in various factories in the early 1960s, but never in sufficient numbers to meet the demands of the Vietcong.

For the Americans, supplies arrived by air or by sea. The Vietcong mostly used trucks for transport. China assisted by providing 16,000 trucks for transportation along the roads which criss-crossed some 12,000 miles across the country and would eventually connect to form a central supply route leading south, running down the spine of the country, which the Americans nicknamed the 'Ho Chi Minh Trail'.

Once this route was identified it became the focus of attention by the US Air Force which sent aircraft to bomb the convoys using it. Trucks produce a lot of dust and at night they can be identified from their 'heat signature' using thermal imaging devices. This made them easy targets. In response the Vietcong resorted increasingly to the use of bicycles loaded with supplies which would be pushed by an army of porters rather than ridden. This was one strategy against which America had little or no effective counter-measure. American 'hi-tech' was about to challenge 'low-tech' and it would not win.

Various methods were tried to counter North Vietnamese insurgency, including a South Vietnamese Militia mounted on bicycles. Some 800 French-made bicycles were obtained and training was given with the intention of operating as local patrols. However, the enterprise collapsed. Lack of enthusiasm was one of the main reasons, but motor vehicles were considered the easier if not better option. As well as Chinese bicycles, the Vietcong used bicycles of various origin including old models produced by Peugeot, and those made in-country at facilities established by engineering concerns such as Thong Nhat, Huu Nghi and Xuan Hoa. They had limited resources available to them but they could repair damaged bicycles and even rebuild machines using parts cannibalised from bicycles too badly damaged to repair. The Czechoslovak-built bicycle known as the 'Favorit' was popular with the Vietcong because of its rugged design. Favorit came out of a company established in 1901, but it had a broken history of production, due to two world wars and coming under Communist influence from 1948. Favorit produced 5,000 machines annually in the early 1950s and 13,500 in 1955. In 1961, 30,000 machines were built, some of which were sent to North Vietnam to be used on the Ho Chi Minh Trail.

As in the wars against the French, the Vietnamese modified their vast fleet of bicycles. They reinforced the forks of the front wheel, attached lengths of bamboo to the handlebars, and removed the saddles. In effect, they transformed the bicycles into wheelbarrows. In some cases, loads of 1,000 pounds were carried. An estimated 200,000 men and women were engaged in this work.

US Military Intelligence was aware of the use of bicycles by the Vietcong. One report noted, 'the employment of bicycle troops is emerging … where the road network is inadequate for motorized transportation, but where paths and dikes may provide an acceptable avenue for bicycle movement.' It noted how useful bicycles could be, citing the Japanese campaign in Malaya and the Vietminh at Dien Bien Phu. The French tried to offer advice about the role of the bicycle, but the Americans quickly dismissed using bicycles themselves. The best answer, as strategists saw it, was to order air strikes against the road network. B-52 bombers dropped hundreds of tons of bombs along the route and smaller aircraft carried out precision bombing against bridges. Results concluded that such operations resulted in a two per cent drop in activity. A more recent analysis estimated that sickness, accidents and snake bites caused a higher rate of attrition to the porters pushing the bicycles, possibly between ten and twenty per cent.

Porters were organised into units along a given stretch of the route. Each man or woman would push their 'pack bikes' for twenty-five miles to a changeover point. There they would hand over their load to the next person in the chain and, if they were lucky, be given a bicycle to ride back to their starting point ready to do it all over again. One unit operating on a stretch of the Ho Chi Minh Trail was the 559th Transport Group with 50,000 troops and a workforce of 100,000 labourers to keep the route in good repair. Two battalions, each with some 2,000 cyclists, were engaged to keep supplies moving along the route. It was like a gigantic relay race which continued day and night, never stopping, and operated in all weathers. If aircraft were heard approaching, the porters simply pushed their bicycles off the tracks and hid under the trees lining the route. If a bridge was destroyed the porters carried their load to the other side. Bomb craters were a minor inconvenience, as were punctures – wheels could be padded with rope. The porters also used foot paths through the jungle. It was slower, perhaps only seven or eight miles per day, but safer.

The Vietcong proved adept at putting their fleet of bicycles to the utmost use, which included illumination for underground hideouts. The lamps remained attached to the bicycle dynamos and the riders would pedal to produce electricity. This was also done in the First World War, but in Vietnam it allowed doctors to treat the wounded in subterranean operating theatres, as in the vast network of tunnels at Cu Chi. The Vietcong also used two bicycles secured together side by side with bamboo poles to evacuate the wounded, also as done in the First World War.

The typical strength of a Vietcong division was around 10,000 men, with daily consumption of three tons of supplies, which equated to either one truck load or seventeen bicycle loads of 400 pounds each. Without this vital line of supply, North Vietnam probably could not have maintained their operations against the US and South Vietnam. In 1968 the movement along the Ho Chi Minh Trail was some 120 tons of supplies daily, with 10–20,000 troops passing along the route each month. The great length of the route meant that it took weeks or even months to go the distance. It was a huge conveyor belt along which men and equipment passed continuously. Much of it was down to the use of the bicycle which the Americans had been so quick to dismiss. Indeed they underrated the Vietcong and the North Vietnamese and in the end paid dearly.

Since the war in Vietnam, many other groups have used bicycles for the same purpose. During the Sri Lankan Civil War of July 1983 to May 2009 the 'Tamil Tigers' used bicycles in operations against government forces.

Bicycles do not always fit into the way civil wars or guerrilla wars are fought, and not all forces see them as necessary items in their arsenal. After more than 140 years of deployment in warfare the use of bicycles is receding, but it has far from disappeared completely from military use. New designs using different materials to produce ultra-lightweight models are now beginning to interest special forces in their ongoing fight against terrorist organizations.

Chapter 17

A Modern Trend

In the twenty-first century there has been increased use of special forces – replacing the 'juggernauts' in fighting wars – executing 'surgical strikes' against precise targets. They have at their disposal a range of technology, including satellites and remotely-controlled drones fitted with cameras. The importance of stealth has led to some units considering the use of bicycles to approach their targets, because of their low noise signatures, size and ease of concealment.

One development, which emerged in the 1970s and 80s, was the sport of 'Mountain Biking' where bicycles were ridden in extreme conditions, off-road and in rugged terrains. Specialist designs were developed to cope with the rough treatment: reinforced frames and wheels; improved braking systems; better tyres, and tyres without inner tubes to reduce or prevent punctures. At first, these machines were just a sporting novelty but, as better designs emerged, some military trials were conducted.

In the early 1990s, Switzerland, with its long-held position of armed neutrality, maintained a dedicated Bicycle Regiment equipped with 5,500 bicycles. They adopted the MO-93, officially known as the Militärrad 93, produced by the company of Condor which had supplied bicycles to the Swiss army for ninety years. The new design was not dissimilar to the old MO-05 it replaced, but it incorporated many innovations, such as improved gears and better braking. It was rugged. It was fitted with carrying racks front and rear. The handlebars mountain-bike style. Additional lighting powered by a dynamo could be fitted to the front rack. Unfortunately it weighed over fifty pounds. In 2001 the Swiss army took the decision to disband the Bicycle Regiment. It has not been replaced, but bicycles are still used in some units of the Swiss army, such as the 17th Fallschirmaufklärer (Parachute Reconnaissance Company 17) a special forces unit based near Locarno. It uses both the MO-93 and the lighter Fahrrad 12, which weighs just over thirty pounds and is also a mountain bike.

The use of bicycles in the Swedish army dates back to 1901 when the Gotland Infantry Regiment was equipped with the Model m/1901 to replace some of its horse-mounted units. Before the Second World War and throughout the conflict Sweden maintained six regiments of bicycle infantry using either the m/30 or m/42 models, along with other types of multi-wheeled design for use as stretcher carriers and radio communications. After the war these regiments were gradually disbanded. Some of the bicycles were placed in storage and later used by *Cykelskyttebataljon* (cyclist battalions) into the 1980s. Others were used by the Home Guard. But Sweden began disposing of its stocks of military bicycles in the 1970s and today has none in service.

The Finnish army still retains some bicycles in service, being used for training conscripts as alternative means of movement, along with skis for adaptability, but motorised vehicles remain the preferred means of transport.

Dutch troops in Afghanistan used bicycles. They were not always service issue but they served the same purpose which was to provide transport to cover more ground faster than possible on foot. It was irregular, but it did produce results, as the Dutch army discovered in Afghanistan between 2006 and 2011. It was decided troops would conduct patrols on bicycles, seeking to gain the confidence of the locals by patrolling with non-military forms of transport. One Dutch officer remembered how the patrols were received by the locals: 'We recently started doing patrols on bicycles in Tarin Kowt. The population was surprised but they reacted positively. It is much easier to come into contact with people on a bicycle than sitting on a Bushmaster [Armoured Personnel Carrier].' British troops in Basra in Iraq also used bicycles.

Modern technology and new materials, such as lightweight alloys and high-impact plastics, have led bicycle manufacturers to develop a range of light and rugged sports machines which have attracted the interest of the military. One example of this crossover from sporting bicycles to military is characterised by the company of Montague, established by father and son Harry and David Montague in 1987 and based in Cambridge, Massachusetts. Their aim was to develop a new range of sports bicycles, including a new design of folding machine, for a modern generation. Both had backgrounds in engineering and design, experiences they combined to develop an innovative range of bicycles such as the 'BiFrame'. Over the next ten years Montague Cycles continued to impress and in 1996 the BMW/Montague Mountain bike was selected as the official machine used for the Olympic Games in Atlanta. This led to interest from the military and in 1997 the company was awarded a two-year grant by the Defense Advanced Research Projects Agency (DARPA) to develop a new bicycle for special roles. One stage of the DARPA project saw Montague working in collaboration with the US Marines to develop a design known as the 'Tactical Electric No Signature' (TENS) Mountain Bike. From it Montague developed a folding design called the 'Paratrooper' Military Mountain Bike, which eliminated the electric power supply and reverted to man power, making it ideal for use by special forces.

The emergence of the Paratrooper folding design continued the tradition of bicycles used by airborne forces, but with the benefit of modern technology and materials. The design is a full-size machine with 26-inch wheels and can be supplied in three sizes of frames, 16, 18 and 20 inches, to suit riders ranging in height from 5′2″ to 6′4″. The idea of providing multiple size frames was originally proposed in 1899 by Baden-Powell during a presentation to the British army. The machine has an aluminium frame to keep the weight down, but even so it still weighs 32 pounds. When collapsed it folds down to fit into a carrying case measuring three feet square which can be attached to a soldier by means of a line to keep it with him during descent. This allows it to land just before the man to reduce impact strain on landing. Once on the ground it takes only thirty seconds to assemble. It has a load carrying capacity of 500 pounds, which is more than sufficient to take the weight of the rider and all his equipment. Riders can attach night vision goggles to their helmets for nocturnal operations, so they do not have to use a light. Montague bicycles are all-terrain machines capable of being used in extreme conditions and climates, from mountains to muddy routes and ice to desert. Already they have been acquired by several military forces and are used by American armed forces in Iraq and Afghanistan.

The next generation of new designs is being developed and already some types have been field tested. Sometimes referred to as 'All Terrain Bikes' (ATB) or 'Extreme Terrain Bikes' (ETB) some have very low profiles and reduced noise levels, exactly as promoted a hundred years ago. Some

ETBs have a design not too dissimilar to that of a wartime motorbike known as a 'Welbike' developed specifically for use by airborne forces, which was a compact machine with a 98hp two-stroke engine capable of 30 mph. The template for many ETB designs appears to be based on this wartime machine. With small, stubby wide tyres the Welbike was collapsible and could be delivered by parachute. Some ETBs have tyres ten inches wide, to reduce ground pressure and perform over all terrains from stony surfaces to sand and mud.

After nearly 140 years in military service, bicycles are still operating in a useful capacity, albeit in a limited way. They were in use before either aircraft or tanks and while they have been overtaken by powerful motorised vehicles they have not been entirely displaced. Armies have become smaller and the special forces using bicycles are also compact units, which means the numbers of bicycles required are also limited. The ways in which they are used has changed over the years and the designs have evolved to meet the changing roles, with the large numbers of the past now being replaced with an emphasis on using fewer numbers more effectively. They have been used by standing national armies, insurgents, resistance groups and all manner of other organizations in time of war. After all this time, there is no reason to believe bicycles should not continue to be used by armies in the future. To have lasted for as long as they have, there must have been much wisdom in their use.

References and Bibliography

Where to see Military Bicycles

The Cobbaton Combat Collection, Chittlehampton, Umberleigh, Devon, EX37 9RZ.

History on Wheels Museum, Longclose House, Common Road, Eton Wick, near Windsor, Berkshire, SL4 6QY.

Memorial du Souvenir a Dunkerque, Courtines du Bastion 32, rue des Chantiers de France, 59140 Dunkerque, France.

The National Cycle Collection, The Automobile Place, Temple Street, Llandrindod Wells, Powys, LD1 5DL.

Mémorial Pegasus, Musée des troupes aéroportées britaniques, Avenue du Major Howard, 14860 Ranville, France.

Walton Hall and Gardens, Walton Lea Road, Higher Walton, Warrington, Cheshire, WA4 6SN.

Some Useful Websites

www.theliberator.be/militarybicycles.htm
www.cobbatoncombat.co.uk
www.historyonwheels.co.uk
www.onlinebicyclemuseum.co.uk
www.questmasters.us/bicycles.html
www.cyclemuseum.org.uk
www.designmuseum.org
www.brooklandsmuseum.com

Bibliography

Ambrose, Stephen E., *The Victors*, Simon & Schuster, London, 2004.
Beevor, Antony, *D–Day; The Battle for Normandy*, Penguin, London, 2010.
Cawthorne, Nigel, *Fighting them on the Beaches*, Arcturus, London, 2002.
Cruickshank, Charles, *The German Occupation of the Channel Islands*, Guernsey, 1991.

Cook, Philip and Shepherd, Ben H, *European Resistance in the Second World War*, Pen & Sword, 2013.

Davis, W.J.K, *German Army Handbook*, Ian Allan, Shepperton, Surrey, 1973.

Deighton, Len, *Blitzkreig*, Jonathan Cape, 1979.

Forty, Simon, *The German Infantryman Operations Manual*, Haynes, Sparkford, 2018.

Greentree, David, *British Paratrooper versus Fallschirmjäger*, Osprey, Oxford, 2013.

Harvey, A.D., *Arnhem*, Cassell, London, 2001.

Hastings, Max, *Overlord: D-Day and the Battle for Normandy 1944*, Pan, London, 2015.

Hastings, Max, *All Hell Let Loose*, Harper, London, 2011.

Hastings, Max, *Armageddon*, Pan Macmillan, London, 2005.

Holmes, Richard, *Tommy: the British Soldier on the Western Front 1914–1918*, Harper Collins, 2004.

Hutchinson, Michael, *Re:Cyclists: 200 Years on Two Wheels*, Bloomsbury, 2018.

Jacmain, L., *Les Diables Noirs: Histoire des Carabiniers Cyclistes*. J&A Janssens, Brussels, 1953.

Kershaw, Robert. J., *It Never Snows in September*, Ian Allan, Shepperton, 1994.

Kirsch, Colin, *Bad Teeth No Bar: A History of Military Cyclists in the Great War*, Unicorn, London 2018.

Kotelnikov, Vladimir, *Red Assault: Soviet Airborne Forces, 1930–1941*, Helion, Warwick, 2019.

Longmate, Norman, *Island Fortress: The Defence of Great Britain 1603–1945*, Grafton, London, 1993.

MacDonald, Lyn, *1914*, Michael Joseph, London, 1987.

Murland, Jerry, *Retreat & Rearguard Dunkirk 1940*, Pen & Sword, 2016.

Sebag-Montefiore, Hugh, *Dunkirk: Fight to the Last Man*, Penguin, London, 2007.

Veranneman, Jean-Michel, *Belgium in the Great War*, Pen & Sword, 2018.

Index

Afghan War, 175
Airborne Troops, Russian, 90–1
Air Raid Precaution (ARP), xi, 125, 127, 129
Alldays Ambulance Bicycle, 76
American Army (AEF) WWI, 84
Anschluss, 92
ANZAC, 51–4
Armentières, France, 52
Army Cyclist Corps (ACC), viii, xii, 29, 60–9, 74, 99
Arnhem, 134, 159–61
Atlantic Wall, 145, 148
Australian Army WWI, 53–4
Australian Light Horse, 51–2
Austro-Prussian War 1866, 6, 10

Baden-Powell, Major Baden Fletcher S., 19–22, 71, 76, 176
Balkan War 1912–1913, 47
Barbarossa, 138
Belgian Army, 26, 106
Bénouville Bridge (Pegasus), 151–2
Benz, Karl, 5
Bersaglieri, 46–7, 117
Bianchi, Edoardo, 10, 46, 87
Bicycle ambulances, 76–9
Birmingham Small Arms (BSA), 3, 22, 51, 129
Blitzkrieg, 95–6, 103, 105
Boer War 1899–1902, x, 8, 18–19, 48, 63
Boy Scouts, 71–2
Brabant's Horse, 19
Bremmer, Colonel, 109
British Airborne Forces, 93, 125, 129, 131
British Expeditionary Force (BEF) 1914, 28–31
Brussels, 158
Buller VC, General Sir Redvers, 23–4
Bund Deutscher Mädel, 98

Canadian Army WWI, 57–60
Canadian Army Cyclists WWI, 50
Carabiniers Cyclists Regiment (Belgian), 32–3
Channel Islands, 113–14, 148
Chasseur Ardennaise, 109–10
Chasseur Cyclist Group, 49
Churchill, Winston, 118
Columbia bicycles, 15, 84
Compax bicycles, 93
Connecticut National Guard, 14
Cornat, General August Victor, 11
Coventry Sewing Machine Company, 2
Cyclists Frontières de Limbourg, 107
Czechoslovakia, industry seized by Germany, 92

Daimler, Gottlieb, 5–6
D-Day, *see* Normandy Landings
Denmark attacked 1940, 106, 111–12
De Witt, General Leon, 31–3
Dickebusch, 42
Dien Bien Phu, 167
Dieppe, 144
Drais, Baron Karl von, 1
Dunkirk, 106, 111–12
Dunlop, John Boyd, 2
Durham, Garnet W., 59
Durkopp Bicycles, 25
Dutch Army, 25–6, 86, 103, 106

Eben Emael, 107
Eden, Antony, 118
Enfield Cycle Company, 23
Extreme Terrain Bikes (ETBs), 176–7

Fahrradbewegliches (Bicycle Infantry Battalion), 148
Fall Gelb (Case Yellow), 103
Finnish Army, 100, 116

Fox, Major G.R., 14
Franco-Prussian War, x, 6, 10, 43

Gallipoli, 51
Girard, Capitaine Henri, 49
German Airborne (*Fallschirmjäger*)
    WWII, 93, 102, 136–7
German army WWI, 69–70
German Bicycle troops WWII, 97
German *Gebirgsjäger* (Mountain troops)
    WWII, 97–8
Germany attacks Belgium 1914, 26
Girl Guides, 71, 125
Gold Beach Normandy, 154–5
Grebbe Line Defences, 103
Gritzner Bicycles, 25
Guderian, General Heinz, 99

Haelen battle, 31–3
Haig, Douglas, 7
Haldane, Lord (Secretary of State for
    War), 14, 62
Haldane Reforms, 14, 63
Harley-Davidson Company, 84–5
Herrenrad Victoria Bicycle, 25, 70
Heydrich, Reinhard, 115
Hill 60, Belgium, xii, 69
Hinckley, Dr John T., 76–7
Hindhaugh, Captain Jacob, 51–2
Hitler, Adolf, 70, 98, 100–101, 115, 138
Ho Chi Minh, 167–8
Ho Chi Minh Trail, 170–3
Hollebeke, 51
Home Guard, xi, 119–22, 175
Hounslow Heath Training Camp, 57, 61–2
Howard, Major John, 152–3
Hungary (Army), 116

Indian army WWI, 50–1
Irish Republic, 3
Italian army WWI, 46–7

Japanese army, 89–90, 138–9
Jeep, 136

Korean War, 168

Lallement, Pierre, 1
Langlois, General Hippolyte, 49

Leitner, Alexander, 10
Lettow-Vorbeck, General Paul von, 55–6
Liddell, Private W., 68
Local Defence Volunteers (LDV), xi,
    118–19

Malaya, 140–1, 143, 167, 172
Market Garden, *see* Arnhem
Maxim, Hiram Percy, 15
McCall, Thomas, 2
Meldegänger (German messengers), 36
Meyer, Eugène, 2
Michaux, Pierre, 1–2
Michelin, 4, 49
Miles, Major General Nelson, 12, 15
Montague Bicycles, 174–6
Moss, Lt James A., 15–17
Munition workers, 74–5
Mussolini, Benito, 46, 89, 91, 116–17

Natali, Lt Luigi Camillo, 46
Neuve Chapelle battle 1915, 7
New Zealand army WWI, 52–3
Normandy Landings, 114, 131, 152–6
Norway attacked 1940, 104

Opel, Adam, 3
Opel Bicycles, 90, 98
Operation Husky, *see* Sicily

Paris, 156–7
Panzerfaust, 151, 162–5
Panzerschreck, 151, 165
Parr, Private John, 34–5
Pashley Bicycles, 4
Pearl Harbor, 136, 140
Peugeot, 2, 4, 49, 168, 171
Pigeons carrying messages, 43–7
Poland attacked 1939, 98
Police forces use of bicycles, 71–2, 125
Polish army, 98
Pope, Lt Col Albert Augustus, 11–12, 15,
    17
Porteous VC, Major Pat, 152
Postal workers, 74, 121
Post Office Rifles, 74
Puch Bicycles, 11

Quadricycles, 5–6, 13, 15

Race to the Sea 1914, 38
Radfahr Kompanies and Battaillonen, 26
Radom Bicycles, 98
Raleigh Bicycle Company, 2
Reichsarbeitsdienst (RAD), x, 98, 116
Reinberger, Major Helmuth, 108–109
Renault, 4
Resistance fighters WWII, 114–15
Reumont 1918, 7
Roger, Émile, 5
Romanian army WWII, 116
Rudge Bicycle Company, 4, 22–3
Russia, 90
Russo-Finnish War 1939, 99
Russo-Japanese War 1904–05, 8

Saipan, 141–3
Savile, Lt Col A.R, 12–13, 22, 76
Sicily, 145
Simms, Frederick Richard, 6
Singapore, 140, 142
Singer Bicycles, 14
Sino-Japanese War, xi
Spalding Bicycle Company, 16
Spanish-American War, 16–17
Spanish Civil War, 91–2, 116
Special Air Service (SAS), 114
Sudan, 16
Swedish army, 86–9, 175
Swiss army, 9, 88, 174
Sword Beach Normandy, 152–3

Tandem cycles, 13
Testafochi, General Eduardo, 46
Theron, Daniel, 19
Tricycles, 4–5, 12–13, 15, 79, 160

US Army WWI, 84–5
US Army WWII, 93
US Airborne Forces WWII, 93, 153, 157–60

Victory bicycles, 93
Vietcong, 168–73
Vietminh, 167–8, 172
Vietnam War, xii, 171–4
Volkssturm, 162–3, 166
Volunteer Cyclists, 13–14, 50, 61
Von Moltke, Helmuth, 6–7
Von Schliefen, Alfred, 6–7

War Car, 6
Wheelmen, 16
Whitby bombarded 1914, 74
Wilson, L/Cpl 'Ginger', 160
Wilson, President Woodrow, 84
Winter War 1939, *see* Russo-Finnish War
Women's Auxiliary Corps, 93
Women's Institute, xi, 125
Women's Land Army, xi, 123–5
Women's Voluntary Service (WVS), xi, 125–6

Xe Tho (Pack Bikes), 168

Yamamoto, Admiral Isoroku, 140
Yokoyama, Lt Colonel Yosuke, 141
Ypres Salient WWI, 59, 69
Yser Canal WWI, 34–5

Zeppelins, 72
Ziegelman, Oberst Fritz, 155
Zillebeke, xii
Zimmerman Telegram, 84